Log Cabins™
For Everyone

Edited by Sandra L. Hatch

HOUSE of
WHITE
BIRCHES
PUBLISHERS
SINCE 1947

Log Cabins for Everyone™

Editorial Director: Vivian Rothe
Editor: Sandra L. Hatch
Associate Editor: Jeanne Stauffer
Assistant Editor: Sue Harvey
Technical Artist: Connie Rand
Copy Editor: Cathy Reef

Photography: Nora Elsesser
Photography Assistant: Linda Quinlan

Production Manager: Vicki Macy
Creative Coordinator: Shaun Venish
Production Artist: Brenda Gallmeyer
Production Coordinator: Sandra Beres
Production Assistants: Carol Dailey, Cheryl Lynch

Publishers: Carl H. Muselman, Arthur K. Muselman
Chief Executive Officer: John Robinson
Marketing Director: Scott Moss

Printed in the United States of America
First Printing: 1996
Library of Congress Number: 96-75670
ISBN: 1-882138-18-X

Every effort has been made to ensure the accuracy and completeness of the instructions in this book. However, we cannot be responsible for human error or for the results when using materials other than those specified in the instructions, or for variations in individual work.

Cover quilts, clockwise from top left:
Dog Cabin Quilt; Triangle Log Cabin; Cutting Corners: Pineapple Block Variation; Antique Courthouse Steps; Miniature Log House; and *Antique Fabric Half-Blocks.*

Quilted Symbols of the Pioneer Spirit

The Log Cabin quilts are considered an American classic. No one knows for sure the exact origin of the design, but the earliest examples date from the 1850s. Many beautiful Log Cabin quilts from the 1880s to the early 1900s survive today.

The Log Cabin name implies a connection to the wood log structure. Each log added to a building secures the previous log while adding size to the foundation. The Log Cabin block shares a similar method of construction, with each fabric strip securing the previous one to create a strong seam.

In the early log cabin structures, the focal point was the fireplace, where meals were cooked and heat was created to warm the cabin. In the Log Cabin block, the chimney is symbolized in the center square. Early Log Cabin quilts had red centers to indicate warmth, or were yellow to symbolize light.

The variations of setting the blocks were symbols as well. The Barn Raising design became recognized as a symbol for the social event surrounding neighbors helping one another construct a barn. Straight Furrows was the ultimate in turning up soil for planting. Courthouse Steps shed light on the quilter's thoughts about the workings of a bureaucracy and the way the courthouse steps were made. A Zigzag pattern represented the fences built to hold animals in.

Although a Log Cabin quilt is made up of individual blocks, it is considered an all-over pattern because one block really can't stand alone. At least four blocks are needed to create a design, just as the early settlers needed one another to survive.

So much symbolism in one simple quilt design! We cannot know for sure how the idea for the first Log Cabin quilt was formed, but we do know it has remained the all-time favorite of quilters and non-quilters to this day.

Much of the fun in making a Log Cabin quilt is planning and laying out the finished blocks. The planning process is the most important. Before you begin to plan for fabric purchases, you need to know the number of blocks in each color arrangement to construct.

We've made it easy for you—all you have to do is open to the page of your favorite Log Cabin design and proceed to purchase the fabrics of your choice.

Because there are many methods of construction and any pattern can be made by any method, the instructions with each quilt will refer you to Pages 144–160. You can use paper-piecing, foundation-piecing, strip-piecing, quilt-as-you-go or template methods for sewing.

Whether you choose a planned color arrangement or scraps in lights and darks to create your pattern, you won't be able to resist making at least one of these wonderful quilts! As you sew, remember the pioneer women as you connect today with the past, making your own symbol of warmth and security.

❧Contents❧

๑Contents๑

Log Cabins for Christmas

Contemporary Log Cabin Quilts

General Instructions

An American Tradition

The romance surrounding the Log Cabin quilt revolves around the pioneer woman living in a log house. No one really knows the beginning of this design, which has continued to be one of the most loved and frequently made quilt designs of all time.

By Xenia Cord

The Log Cabin design in quiltmaking has long been a source of pride, practicality and playfulness, its seemingly endless variations presenting a visual treat. Although the origins of the Log Cabin design are not clear, its stripped arrangement, centering a square of unifying colors, has long been an icon of American pride.

When cotton and batting were scarce during the Civil War, quilters pressed wool on foundation as in the Straight Furrows quilt.

The pioneer period, existing as it did in overlapping decades as the frontier moved westward, is most identified by the log cabin in architecture, and is echoed by the quilt design of the same name. And Abraham Lincoln, political leader, president and poignant symbol of a pivotal period in American history, is strongly associated with the log cabin image. Surviving antique quilts in variations of the Log Cabin design suggest that the 1860s was a time when the pattern enjoyed great popularity, especially in the North.

The basic color arrangement of a block constructed of half dark and half light strips of fabric, or solid color strips on half and multi-prints on the other, allowed for creative arrangements that led to popular variations with their own names. Most were reminiscent of the pioneer experience: Straight Furrow, Sunshine and Shadow, Barn Raising, Streak of Lightning.

Quartering or further dividing of the block into light and dark, and varying the sequence in which the strips were attached, led to complex and decorative sets such as Courthouse Steps, Pineapple and Windmill Blades. Other formations were created by changing the center figure to a hexagon, diamond or triangle and building outward accordingly.

Constructed in two different ways, Log Cabins allowed the quiltmaker to employ straight cutting of narrow strips, resulting in little waste. In the 1860s when cotton fabric and batting were scarce in the North because of the Civil War, Log Cabin quilts were often made of wool strips secured to a foundation, and were called "pressed" quilts. Straight-cut strips of wool will ravel; with one free edge stitched down onto a foundation of any available fabric, and then finger-pressed over and the next strip sewed facedown on top of the remaining free edge and so on, seams were subject to less stress in the finished composition.

Foundation-pieced compositions also did not require cotton batting. Only the seams joining the blocks were completed by seaming with the right sides together. A fabric back was added; quilting, decorative ties, or hidden tacks at the block intersections and centers completed the composition. The second construction technique involved the more familiar seamed construction, sewing the strips to each other without any foundation. These designs were batted and backed in traditional ways and unified by quilting.

Two quilts in this section are pressed quilts. The first is a Straight Furrow variation made by Margaret Jane Neely (1834–1932) of Juniata County, Pa., in the 1860s. Constructed of wool on the front, with wool twill tape binding, the quilt is pressed on foundation and quilted only in the seams around each block.

The non-traditional color of the center squares is Prussian blue, a color associated with Pennsylvania quilts throughout the 19th century. The rich variety of printed wool dress and cape fabrics, and the mauvine print back (now

Windmill Blades has 81 pieces in each 4 1/2" block, a total of 9,477 logs 1/4" wide. The inset shows the size of the strips compared to a small scissors.

faded to brown) suggests a late 1860s date, and reminds us that some quiltmakers remained affluent regardless of the economics required by the Civil War.

The second pressed quilt uses only two fabrics in its construction, and is from the last quarter of the 19th century. A Victorian impulse toward excess, and the desire to fit as much as possible into the design space, led to quilts with tiny pieces. The Windmill Blades quilt, in wine red wool and olive green and black plaid silk, is constructed of 3/4" cut strips, with 81 pieces in each 4 1/2" block.

There are 9,477 logs 1/4" wide in the design area, all pieced on foundation without the benefit of pre-marked guidelines! The 9" borders of olive wool challis and a back of brown cotton skirt lining complete the 56" x 74" quilt.

Because the borders are unsupported and the center on foundation is dense and heavy, there is reason to believe that this quilt was meant to be displayed over a parlor sofa, or perhaps a

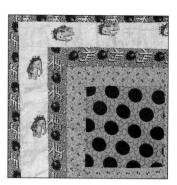

The "conversation prints" in Related Square are oriental motifs, a result of Far East trade in the late 1800s. Examples are the oriental couple and elephants shown.

piano. Certainly the unknown Ohio quiltmaker who created this tour de force deserves admiration (courtesy of the Kalona Quilt & Textile Museum, where it is on loan from Woodlin Wheel Antiques, Kalona, Iowa).

At the American Centennial Exposition in Philadelphia in 1876, among the most exciting exhibits were those in the pavilions or halls of the Orient, which were widely popular because they offered to the West new and hitherto unseen cultures. Japan had been opened to Western trade by the forceful negotiations of Adm. Matthew Perry which concluded in March of 1854; similar military action by France and England had resulted in the opening of China to economic and religious missions by 1860.

Their popular international exhibits in Philadelphia led to general interest in oriental design; this fascination led fabric manufacturers to create "conversation prints" in oriental motifs. The cotton top shown here is a Log Cabin/ Related

Square, pieced on foundation and consisting almost entirely of oriental motif prints.

The block centers and setting fabric are a pseudo-oriental character print, and the floral outer border shows coins with foreign lettering. Conversation prints include howdah-laden elephants with small passengers, and oriental couples in kimonos, carrying parasols. It is possible that the unknown quiltmaker was memorializing in fabric her trip to the Centennial Exposition.

By the 20th century, foundation construction of Log Cabins appears to have been abandoned for the more familiar pieced technique, with its requisite batting, back and quilting. Quilting presented somewhat of a design dilemma; a quilt with numerous seams means quilting must pass through additional layers of fabric.

Quilters often solved this problem by quilting a line through the center of each log, turning the corner to the log at right angles, and creating mazelike figures when the quilt is viewed from the back. Other quilters created the same figure by quilting in the ditch, the seam between the strips. Another way to quilt in continuous lines was to mark a repetitive design unrelated to the pattern of the top. Baptist Fans, drawn in repeated arcs at regular intervals, was such a design.

By accident or design, the Lawrenceburg, Ill., quiltmaker who made the blocks for the 1920s

Courthouse Steps made several different kinds of sets. This is an amusing quilt to look at, because not all the blocks do the expected, and the variation is visually interesting.

While most of the blocks are set in alternate quarters of light and dark, the use of less contrasting fabrics creates some blocks that vary the regularity of the design. And a few of the blocks in this all-print composition are set half light and half dark, leading the eye over the surface again and again in an attempt to understand the design.

The Barn Raising quilt made by Rosa Detwiler of Burnettsville, Ind., in the 1920s attracts the eye for another reason. Carefully constructed in cottons, the blocks are intended to create a balanced, orderly look. Although the quilt is square, the number of blocks has resulted in an asymmetrical, visually intriguing design. The light and dark shirtings, in indigo prints, soldier or cadet blues, shaker grays and wine prints are complemented by pastel plaids, ginghams, stripes and chambrays (and no florals).

There are 25 blocks in the quilt, set five by five. The center block is all pastel, and the remainder are light and dark. While Barn Raising usually requires a square design field, it cannot be accomplished with only 25 blocks, so Rosa's barn tilts a little. Her planned quilt has borders and back in a single blue-and-white plaid.

The design variations possible from a basic construction requiring straight cutting with little waste and straight-line sewing easily accomplished with only simple sewing skills allowed generations of quiltmakers to play with color, shading and surface design as they made practical and decorative quilts. More sophisticated quiltmakers also manipulated fabric shapes and added elements to the basic block, creating permutations in cloth that continue to challenge and inspire today's quiltmaker.

Notice all the variations in these Courthouse Steps blocks. We'll never know whether or not they were planned that way.

Not having enough blocks for a regular Barn Raising setting resulted in the quilter creating this intriguing asymmetrical design.

From Sandra L. Hatch

Antique
Log Cabin Quilts

The Log Cabin quilt may be the most-loved and most often made quilt of all times. In the pioneer days it was popular because small, straight-cut strips could be utilized to create blocks that required minimal sewing skills.

Today quiltmakers still search for ways to make the Log Cabin in yet more challenging designs that use the same simple methods of cutting and sewing as our predecessors.

As you create your own version of your favorite Log Cabin set and design, you will feel connected to the generations of quiltmakers who came before you.

Triangle Log Cabin

Even though the Log Cabin blocks used in this quilt are almost like those used in several other quilts, there is a minor change which affects the design. Instead of a square center, two triangles are used. In this setting, the lights and darks make a straight line design at the break instead of the jagged line formed when a square is used.

This antique *Triangle Log Cabin* quilt is another example of how a quilter can change one tiny element of a design to create a different effect. Here, the center of the block is not a square, as was typical in most early versions. The square has been divided into two triangles—one light side and one red side. The maker stuck to tradition where the red center is concerned, but not completely.

Changing the square to two triangles does change the design formed when the blocks are arranged in the Barn Raising design as shown. The light side of the design is completely separated from the dark side. In a traditional Log Cabin in the Barn Raising design, the red center square breaks up that light/dark color and makes a jag in the design as shown in Figure 1.

Look at the close-up photo of one block in Figure 5. Notice that every other round on each side uses the same fabric. This makes a more planned color arrangement than some scrap Log Cabins. Also note that the shorter strip always starts on the white triangle side to create the pattern.

We wonder about the history of this quilt. It contains some conversation prints like those used on the *Antique Courthouse Steps* on Page 21. Because the fabrics aren't quite as bright and new looking, they don't show up as much.

Quilt Specifications

Skill Level: Easy   **Quilt Size:** 100" x 100"
Block Size: 10" x 10"   **Number of Blocks:** 100

Materials

- 3 3/4 yards dark print scraps
- 3 1/8 yards light print scraps
- 1/3 yard each red solid and muslin
- Backing 104" x 104"
- Batting 104" x 104"
- All-purpose thread to match fabrics
- 11 1/4 yards self-made or purchased binding

We can tell the quilt was used. It also has a hole all the way through, which we think was made by a mouse! The hole could be patched, but it gives the quilt personality and we like it just the way it is!

Instructions

Step 1. Cut red and muslin triangles using the template given on Page 15.

Step 2. Cut all remaining fabrics into 1 1/2"-wide strips.

Step 3. Sew a red solid and muslin triangle together to make a square. Repeat for 100

Triangle Log Cabin
Placement Diagram
100" x 100"

Figure 1
If a solid square were used in the center, the Barn Raising design would be broken up as shown.

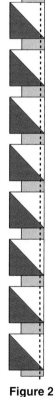

Figure 2
Sew the stitched unit onto a light print strip as shown.

squares. Press seams toward the red solid triangle.

Step 4. Place the pieced squares on a light print strip with muslin triangle side even with the edge of the strip; sew, adding triangle/ squares to strip as you sew referring to Figure 2 and Page 149 for fast-piecing instructions.

Step 5. Press and cut segments even with triangle/squares referring to Figure 3.

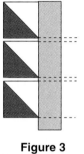

Figure 3
Cut strip even with square as shown.

Step 6. Using another strip of the same print, place the stitched unit onto the strip with the second muslin side even with the edge of the strip as shown in Figure 3; sew as for first strip. Press and trim even referring to Figure 4.

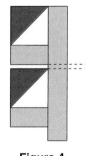

Figure 4
Trim off strip even with first segment as shown.

Step 7. Sew a dark strip to each red solid side of the center unit in the same manner.

Continue adding strips, repeating the same fabrics in every other round on both the light and dark sides, referring to the block piecing diagram to create the pattern. Repeat for 100 blocks.

Step 8. Square up blocks to 10 1/2" x 10 1/2".

Step 9. Arrange the blocks in 10 rows of 10 blocks each referring to the Placement Diagram. Join the blocks in rows; press. Join the rows to complete the top; press.

Step 10. Sandwich batting between completed top and prepared backing piece. Safety-pin or baste layers together to hold flat.

Step 11. Finish quilt in chosen method referring to Pages 152–160.

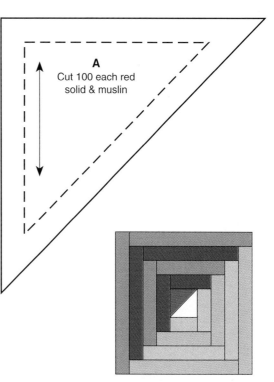

A
Cut 100 each red solid & muslin

Triangle Log Cabin
10" x 10" Block

Figure 5
This close-up of 1 block shows how the red x fabric strip is pieced to make it large enough to be used.

Tips & Techniques

Quilters from the 19th century used every scrap to create their quilts. If a piece wasn't quite large enough, it could be sewn together with another scrap of the same fabric to make it fit. Notice in Figure 5 that there is a seam in the last pink strip to make it fit. This seam is barely visible. Today we might not be so frugal and would be afraid someone would call this inventive technique a mistake!

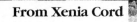
From Xenia Cord

Zigzag Log Cabin

This beautiful and unusual Log Cabin quilt was made in 1888 in Burlington, Ind.
It is inscribed "Eli Robards" and "1888" in the center. The quilt was probably
made by Eli's mother as an Emancipation Quilt when he turned 21 that year.

The *Zigzag Log Cabin* is a wonderful catalog of fabrics from the 1880s and is another example of the positive/negative design formed when one side of the Log Cabin block is made from all-white solid fabric while the opposite side is completed with a variety of medium and dark print strips. Emancipation Quilts were common in the 19th century.

Instructions

Step 1. Cut two strips white solid 2" x 81 1/2" along the lengthwise grain of the fabric. Cut all remaining fabrics (except navy blue print strips) into 1 1/4"-wide strips.

Step 2. If using template method, prepare templates referring to instructions on Page 145 and using the full-size block drawing given in Figure 1 on Page 18. If using foundation- or paper-piecing methods, make 252 copies of the full-size drawing and refer to Page 150 for instructions for completing blocks.

Step 3. If using the strip-piecing method, sew a white strip (***Note:*** *Use the white strips cut from the full width of fabric, not from the area used to cut long border strips.*) to a solid red strip; repeat for eight strips. Cut each strip unit into 1 1/4" segments—36 per strip.

Step 4. Sew these segments to a print strip with the white square toward the back of the

Quilt Specifications

Skill Level: Intermediate
Quilt Size: 67 1/2" x 81"
Block Size: 4 1/2" x 4 1/2"
Number of Blocks: 252

Materials

- 3 1/2 yards print scraps in medium and dark colors
- 3 1/2 yards white solid
- 1/3 yard red solid
- 2 strips navy blue print 1 1/4" x 81 1/2"
- Backing 71" x 85"
- Batting 71" x 85"
- All-purpose thread to match fabrics
- 9 yards self-made or purchased binding

machine referring to Figure 2.

Step 5. Press and cut strips even with the white/red segments referring to Figure 3.

Step 6. Sew a white strip to the opposite side of the segments as shown in Figure 4. Press and trim strip even with segment.

Step 7. Continue to add strips in numerical order as shown in Figure 5. Keep dark colors on one side of the center and white on the other side.

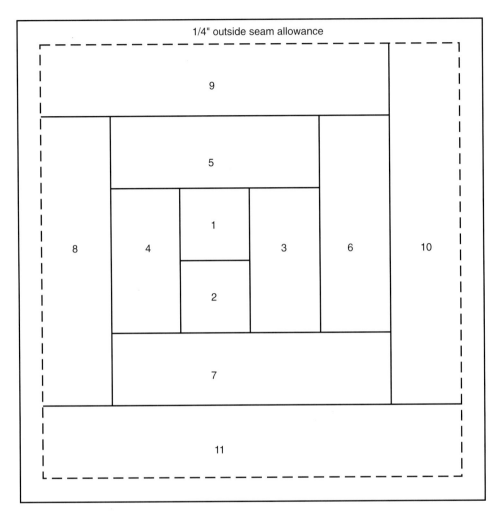

Figure 1
Use this full-size block drawing as a foundation pattern or to make full-size templates for individual pieces.
Note: Remember the design is reversed as this pattern would be the wrong side of the block.

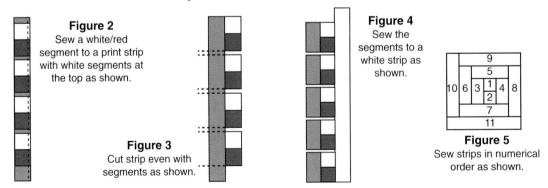

Figure 2
Sew a white/red segment to a print strip with white segments at the top as shown.

Figure 3
Cut strip even with segments as shown.

Figure 4
Sew the segments to a white strip as shown.

Figure 5
Sew strips in numerical order as shown.

Step 8. Complete 252 blocks. Press and square up blocks to 5" x 5".

Step 9. Arrange the blocks in 18 rows of 14 blocks each, referring to the Placement

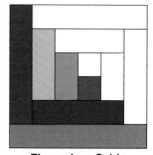
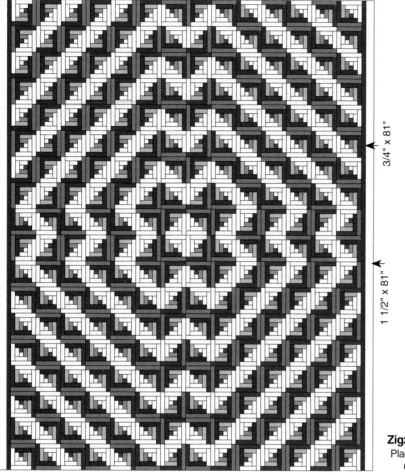

3/4" x 81"

1 1/2" x 81"

Zigzag Log Cabin
4 1/2" x 4 1/2" Block

Zigzag Log Cabin
Placement Diagram
67 1/2" x 81"

Diagram for block placement. Join the blocks in rows; press. Join the rows to complete the top; press.

Step 10. Sew navy blue print strips to the long sides of the quilt center; press seams toward strips.

Step 11. Sew the white strips cut in Step 1 to the long side of the quilt center; press seams toward strips.

Step 12. Sandwich batting between completed top and prepared backing piece. Safety-pin or baste layers together to hold flat.

Step 13. Finish quilt in chosen method referring to Pages 152–160.

Did You Know?

Emancipation, also called Freedom Quilts were made by friends and relatives for a young man when he reached the legal age of 21. This age represented the time when he was no longer required to give all earned wages to his father and that if he had been an apprentice, he was free to begin work on his own. This was a time of celebration, and there would be a party for him with his friends as guests. He was presented with his Freedom Quilt, which usually had subjects of masculine interest. The quilt was most often stored away until the young man married, at which time the quilt was presented to his bride as a gift.

From Sandra L. Hatch

Antique Courthouse Steps

Although it is over 100 years old, the fabrics in this Courthouse Steps look as crisp and new as if they were bought yesterday. If you could examine the blocks closely, you would find some interesting prints, which we call conversation prints today.

According to *Textile Designs* by Susan Meller and Joost Elffers (Harry Abrams Inc., 1991) conversation prints depict some real creature or object—something we recognize. In this quilt, many conversation prints are recognizable: dogs, suits of playing cards, planets, fireworks and more.

In the latter part of the 19th century, mill engravings (prints made with copper rollers engraved with a design transferred from a small steel roller called a "mill") were extremely popular. Usually these prints were made using only two colors—red and black—on a white shirting-weight background.

If you are a textile enthusiast, this quilt will delight you with many typical fabrics from the 1880s. Examining each print and comparing it to photos of fabrics from textile books showing different time periods is a wonderful pastime.

If you are only interested in duplicating this quilt with today's fabrics, look for contemporary novelty or conversation prints and see how much fun it can be for others to find them in your finished quilt.

Quilt Specifications

Skill Level: Easy **Quilt Size:** 72" x 72"
Block Size: 9" x 9"
Number of Blocks: 64

Materials

- 2 yards dark print scraps
- 3 yards light print scraps
- 3 strips red solid 1 1/2" x 45"
- Backing 76" x 76"
- Batting 76" x 76"
- All-purpose thread to match fabrics
- 8 1/4 yards self-made or purchased binding

Instructions
Step 1. Cut all fabrics into 1 1/2"-width strips.

1 1/2"

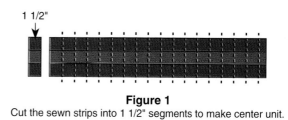

Figure 1
Cut the sewn strips into 1 1/2" segments to make center unit.

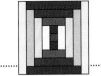

Step 2. Sew a dark strip to each side of each red solid strip; press seams away from red strip. Cut both strips into 1 1/2" segments as shown in Figure 1. You will need 64 segments.

Step 3. Sew a light strip to each side of the 1 1/2" segments, using fast-piecing methods on Page 149, and referring to Figure 2.

Step 4. Press and cut strips even with center segment.

Step 5. Continue adding light and dark strips to opposite sides of the center strip as shown in Figure 3 until you have four rows on each side of the center. Complete 64 blocks.

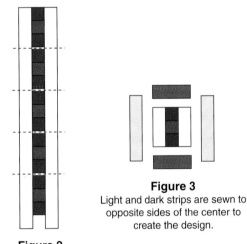

Figure 3
Light and dark strips are sewn to opposite sides of the center to create the design.

Figure 2
Sew light strips to each side of the center and trim even with center segments as shown.

Step 6. Press and square up blocks to 9 1/2" x 9 1/2".

Step 7. Arrange the blocks in eight rows of eight blocks each referring to the Placement Diagram. Join the blocks in rows; press. Join the rows to complete the top; press.

Step 8. Sandwich batting between completed top and prepared backing piece. Safety-pin or baste layers together to hold flat.

Step 9. Finish quilt in chosen method referring to Pages 152–160.

Figure 4
The fabrics used in this quilt are perfect examples of conversation prints from the late 1800s.

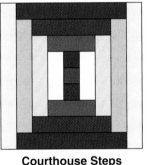

Courthouse Steps
9" x 9" Block

Tips & Techniques

The Courthouse Steps design makes a beautiful scrap quilt. It is a good idea to use the same fabric, for each side on each round and to keep light and dark sides. Foundation paper or fabric may be used to create accurate blocks, but is not necessary. The quilt shown has some obvious wide and narrow strips, yet all the blocks fit together to make a perfectly beautiful quilt.

Courthouse Steps
Placement Diagram
72" x 72"

From Xenia Cord

Positive/Negative Barn-Raising Log Cabin

It will take you some time to create a copy of this beautiful quilt. The quilt shown was made by Asa Mable Johnson from Selma, Ind., in 1953. It includes a wonderful assortment of scraps from the 1930s and 1940s.

The Log Cabin block used in this *Positive/ Negative Barn Raising* variation is unique because its center starts out like a Courthouse Steps block but the rest of the block is completed in the traditional Log Cabin rounds. There is no center square, and without this, the center of the block is not defined; thus the viewer sees floating white and mixed-print diamonds in a positive/negative effect.

In addition to the fact that the quilt includes 396 blocks using 5/8" finished logs, the quilt was hand-pieced and hand-quilted through the center of each log.

Although the maker did not use fast-piecing techniques, they can be used to complete this quilt just like all others. Even though we can't imagine anyone wanting to hand-piece a quilt like this, we are sharing a full-size drawing of the block. You may use the drawing to make copies for foundation piecing or to create templates for individual pieces.

Instructions

Step 1. Cut two strips white solid 1 1/4" x 69 1/2" and two strips 1 1/4" x 84 1/2" along the lengthwise grain of the fabric. Cut all remaining fabrics into 1 1/8"-wide strips.

Step 2. If using template method, prepare templates referring to instructions on Page 145 and

Quilt Specifications

Skill Level: Intermediate
Quilt Size: 69" x 84"
Block Size: 3 3/4" x 3 3/4"
Number of Blocks: 396

Materials

- 4 1/4 yards print scraps in medium and dark colors
- 3 3/4 yards white solid
- 1/2 yard red solid
- Backing 73" x 88"
- Batting 73" x 88"
- All-purpose thread to match fabrics
- 9 yards self-made or purchased binding

using the full-size block drawing given in Figure 1 on Page 26. If using foundation-piecing methods, make 396 copies of the full-size drawing and refer to Page 150 for instructions for completing blocks.

Step 3. If using the strip-piecing method, sew a white strip (***Note:*** *Use the white strips which were cut from the full width of fabric, not from the area used to cut long border strips.*) to a red strip; repeat for 11 strips. Cut each strip into 1 1/8" segments—39 per strip.

Step 4. Sew these segments to a print strip

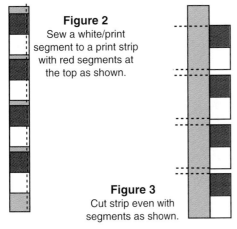

with the red square toward the back of the machine referring to Figure 2.

Figure 2
Sew a white/print segment to a print strip with red segments at the top as shown.

Figure 3
Cut strip even with segments as shown.

Step 10. Sandwich batting between completed top and prepared backing piece. Safety-pin or baste layers together to hold flat.

Step 11. Finish quilt in chosen method referring to Pages 152–160.

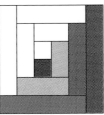

Positive/Negative Barn Raising
3 3/4" x 3 3/4" Block

Step 5. Press and cut strips even with the white/print segments referring to Figure 3.

Step 6. Continue sewing segments to strips in the color order shown in the piecing diagram. One side of each block has all white rounds; the other side has print rounds.

Step 7. Complete 396 blocks. Press and square up blocks to 4 1/4" x 4 1/4".

Step 8. Arrange the blocks in 22 rows of 18 blocks each, referring to the Placement Diagram for block placement. Join the blocks in rows; press. Join the rows to complete the top; press.

Step 9. Sew white strips cut in Step 1 to each side of the quilt center, mitering corners; press completed top.

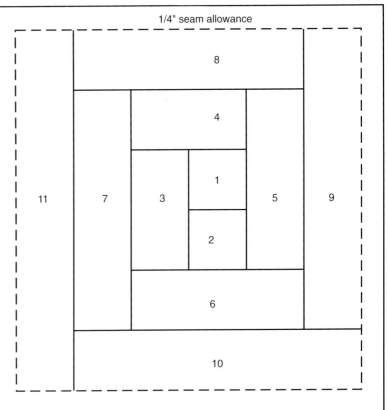

1/4" seam allowance

Figure 1
Use this full-size block drawing as a foundation pattern or to make full-size templates for individual pieces.
Note: *Remember the design is reversed as this pattern would be the wrong side of the block.*

3/4" x 69" ↓

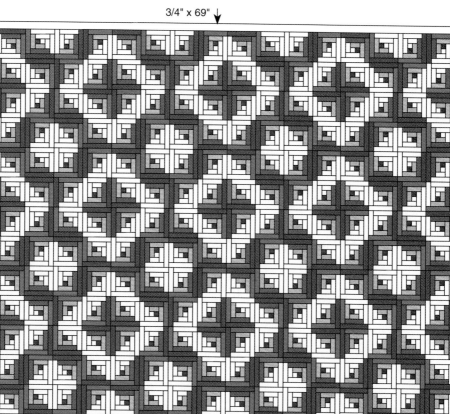

3/4" x 84"

Positive/Negative Barn Raising Log Cabin
Placement Diagram
69" x 84"

From Xenia Cord

Hexagonal Comfort

A hexagonal center surrounded by 37 fabric strips creates the design formed on this unusual comforter. The blocks were hand-pieced on foundations. The fabrics are printed and woven wools, wool challis and silk. The back is a brown, cream and madder print chintz. Printed on the back among the flowers is the name "Marie Howard." Circa 1860–1880, this quilt was found in Indiana.

Most 19th century Log Cabin quilts were pieced on foundation fabric and were tied rather than quilted. The basic reason for this is obvious—backing, batting, foundation and top fabrics form a very heavy layer, too heavy to make neat quilting stitches through.

This comforter is heavy. The hexagon centers have purple or yellow wool ties which hold the layers together.

It would be difficult to reproduce this quilt exactly as is shown. However, the pattern is interesting and would create a challenge for most quilters.

Instructions

Step 1. If using template method, prepare templates referring to instructions and using the full-size block drawing given in Figure 1 on Page 32 .

Step 2. If using foundation- or paper-piecing methods, make 126 copies of the full-size drawing and refer to Page 150 for instructions for completing blocks.

Step 3. Cut 126 red hexagons for center using full-size hexagon in the center of Figure 1 (add seam allowance when cutting).

Step 4. Cut all remaining fabrics into 1"-wide strips.

Quilt Specifications

Skill Level: Challenging
Quilt Size: Approximately 67 1/2" x 80"
Block Size: 7 1/4" x 8 3/8"
Number of Blocks: 126 (94 whole blocks, 22 partial blocks and 10 half-blocks)

Materials

- 3 yards medium-color print scraps
- 3 yards black solid
- 3 yards light print scraps
- 1/3 yard red solid
- Backing 72" x 84"
- Batting 72" x 80"
- All-purpose thread to match fabrics
- 8 1/2 yards self-made or purchased binding

Step 5. If using the foundation- or paper-piecing methods, place the red hexagon on the

Figure 2
Complete 22 partial blocks using blue dotted line on Figure 1 (add seam) as a guide.

Figure 3
Complete 10 half-blocks for top and bottom using red dotted line on Figure 1 (add seam) as a guide.

center. Sew a black strip to opposite sides, referring to the numbers on the full-size pattern in Figure 1 for order of piecing.

Step 6. Continue adding segments to opposite sides of the center in numerical order, pressing after each addition, adding 37 strips to center in all. ***Note:*** *If making partial and half-blocks, refer to dotted lines on Figure 1 for guidance in placing strips.*

Step 7. Complete 94 whole blocks, 22 partial blocks (Figure 2) and 10 half-blocks (Figure 3).

Make a template the size of the finished block plus a 1/4" seam allowance all around. Trim all blocks to fit this template to make all blocks a uniform size. Repeat for partial and half-blocks.

Step 8. Arrange 11 whole blocks in vertical rows as shown in Figure 4; join together to make a row. Repeat for four rows; press. Arrange 10 whole blocks with a half-block on the top and bottom as shown in Figure 5; join together to make a row. Repeat for five rows; press. Arrange 11 partial blocks in vertical rows as shown in Figure 6; join together to make a row. Repeat for opposite side; press.

Step 9. Join the rows to complete the quilt center; press. ***Note:*** *If you chose to complete whole blocks and trim after stitching, join the blocks in vertical rows and sew together. Trim edges even after pressing.*

Step 10. Sandwich batting between completed top and prepared backing piece. Safety-pin or baste layers together to hold flat.

Step 11. Finish quilt in chosen method referring to Pages 152–160.

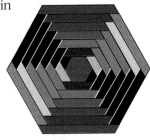

Hexagonal Comfort
7 1/4" x 8 3/4"

Figure 4	**Figure 5**	**Figure 6**
Make 4 rows using whole blocks as shown.	Make 5 rows using whole and half-blocks as shown.	Make 1 of each row as shown for sides of quilt using partial blocks.

Tips & Techniques

Sometimes it is easier to piece complete blocks which are trimmed after they are sewn together than it is to try to sew half- and partial blocks. If you don't want to waste fabric and time to piece areas of the blocks that will just get trimmed off, use the full-size pattern with marked lines as guides to create blocks with only the areas needed to complete the blocks filled with fabric.

Hexagonal Comfort
Placement Diagram
Approximately 67 1/2" x 80"

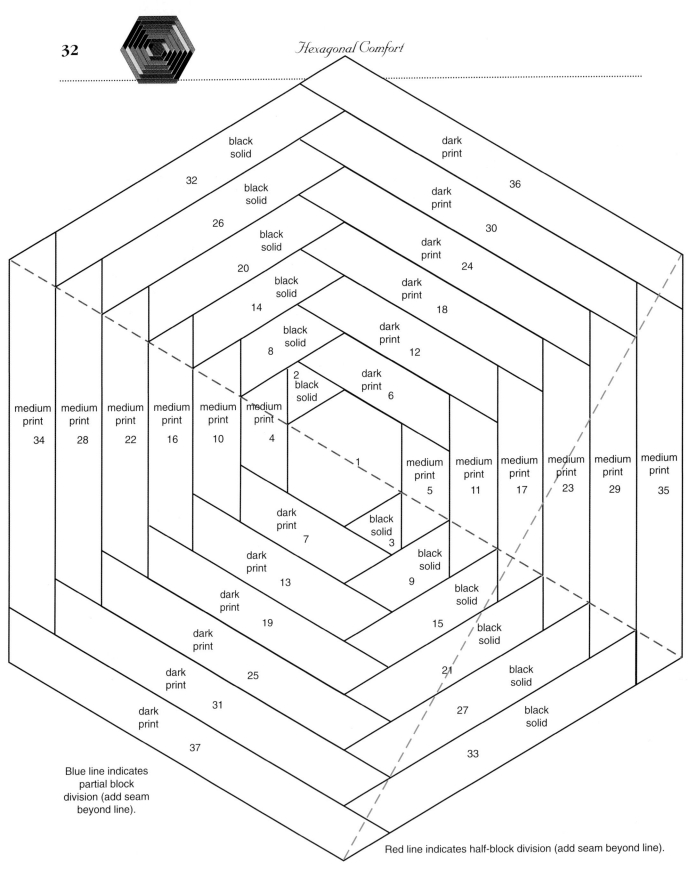

Figure 1
Use this full-size block drawing as a foundation pattern or to make full-size templates for individual pieces. Dotted lines indicate right and left edge blocks and top and bottom edge blocks. ***Note:*** *Remember the design is reversed as this pattern would be the wrong side of the block.*

Log Cabin Gallery

The *Log Cabin* design is so versatile that through the selection of color and the setting chosen you can match any decor and create any mood. This splendid *Chinese Lantern* quilt uses the Courthouse Steps design and color placement to create the look of Oriental lanterns.

By Mary Jane Lamphier

Traditional
Log Cabin Quilts

Now that you have seen a few quilts from earlier times, you might like to see some of the traditional patterns that have been made more recently. These quilts may be creative or quite typical of classic designs, but all of them are easy to make. Some use scraps while others have planned color arrangements.

Regardless of the outcome of the design, the basic technique of building around a center design to create a block or quilt is still integral to the construction process.

If you prefer more traditional projects both in methods and fabrics, we know you will have fun with these versatile quilts!

Wagon Wheel

"I don't have time to quilt." "I don't have the patience." "Hand-sewing isn't my thing." Have you heard these comments from your non-quilting friends? Yes, we know quilting isn't for everyone, but if there is a quilt that almost anyone can make, it is the Log Cabin.

The quilt shown was made in the quilt-as-you-go method and uses three different color variations in the blocks to create the *Wagon Wheel* design. Traditionally the center of most antique Log Cabin quilts was red or yellow. This quilt is no exception. As with traditional blocks, the blocks used here have a dark and light side, except for the center of the block, which is made with all one color.

The design of this Log Cabin is formed from the use of three block variations. Arranging them as shown in the Placement Diagram creates a design we call Wagon Wheel. Although it looks complicated, creating the design is easy.

The sample was stitched in the quilt-as-you-go method described on Page 150. Use this or other preferred methods to make the blocks. No matter what method you choose, the design will not be affected. It is the arrangement of the blocks which creates the design.

Instructions

Step 1. Cut three strips red mini-dot 2" by fabric width.

Step 2. Cut remaining fabrics into 2" by fabric width strips.

Step 3. Sew a red strip to a medium green strip three times; press and cut into 2" segments as

Quilt Specifications

Skill Level: Intermediate
Quilt Size: 108" x 108"
Block Size: 13 1/2" x 13 1/2"
Number of Blocks: 64

Materials

- 1/4 yard brick red mini-dot
- 6 yards medium green print
- 3 yards dark green print
- 1 yard light print
- Backing 112" x 112"
- Batting 112" x 112"
- All-purpose thread to match fabrics
- 12 yards self-made or purchased binding

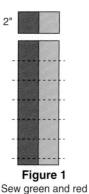

Figure 1
Sew green and red strips together. Cut into 2" segments.

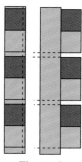

Figure 2
Sew center segment to medium green strip as shown.

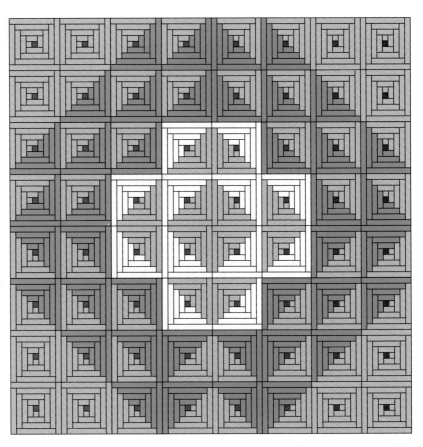

shown in Figure 1. You will need 64 segments. ***Note:*** *If you use quilt-as-you-go methods described on Page 150, prepare batting and backing squares as described; mark to find the centers. Place the 2" segments in the center of the squares and sew the strips in the manner described. Refer to figure drawings to create the correct color versions.*

Step 4. If using fast-piecing methods described on Pages 149 and 150, beginning with Block 1, sew 40 of the 2" segments to medium green strips referring to Figure 2. Press and cut strips even with segments. Continue adding strips, referring to Figure 3 for color placement for Block 1. Complete 40 Block 1 squares; press.

Step 5. Repeat the piecing process referring to Figure 4 to complete 12 Block 2 squares; press.

Step 6. Repeat the piecing process referring to Figure 5 to complete 12 Block 3 squares; press.

Figure 3
Piece 40 Block 1 squares as shown.

Figure 4
Piece 12 Block 2 squares as shown.

Figure 5
Piece 12 Block 3 squares as shown.

Step 7. When all blocks are complete, arrange in eight rows of eight blocks each referring to the Placement Diagram for pattern arrangement.

Wagon Wheel
Placement Diagram
108" x 108"

Color Key
☐ Light print
▨ Dark green print
☐ Medium green print
▨ Brick red mini-dot

Wagon Wheel Block
13 1/2" x 13 1/2"

Step 8. Join the blocks in rows. ***Note:*** *If using quilt-as-you-go methods, refer to Page 150 for sewing blocks together and joining rows to complete quilt.*

Step 9. Join the rows to complete quilt top; press.

Step 10. Finish quilt in chosen method referring to Pages 152–160.

By Mary Curry

Using Drapery Fabrics

Stripes and heavy drapery fabric together in a Log Cabin quilt? Why not? Because the fabric used in this quilt was so heavy, it could not be quilted by hand. It was machine-quilted on one of those large machines using a precut design. It is a very heavy and warm quilt, which is much appreciated during the winter months.

You don't need to be hung up on what type of fabrics to use in Log Cabin quilts. Our predecessors used anything they had on hand—wool, silks and cottons; prints, solids and stripes. You might consider looking in the drapery and upholstery departments of your local fabric store for bargain remnants or yardage to match your home's decor.

Don't limit your fabric choices to what you think should be used, but try not to mix different fabric weights in the same quilt. For example, don't use a heavy chintz print with a silk noile.

Instructions

Step 1. Cut off-white chintz into strips 2 1/2" by fabric width.

Step 2. Cut striped fabric lengthwise on the stripes in 2 1/2" widths, trying to stay within stripe on each strip.

Step 3. Cut one lengthwise strip print for centers 2 1/2" by fabric length. Sew off-white chintz strips to the long print strip; press and cut in 2 1/2" segments. You will need 42 of these segments for centers of blocks.

Step 4. Using speed-piecing methods provided on Page 149, complete 42 blocks referring to

Quilt Specifications

Skill Level: Easy   **Quilt Size:** 90" x 90"
Block Size: 14" x 14"
Number of Blocks: 42

Materials

- 4 yards off-white with gold metallic print chintz
- 5 yards striped drapery fabric (stripe should be 2 1/2" wide to confine design in strips for logs; yardage allows for no waste)
- 3 yards matching print for centers and border strips (allows cutting lengthwise border strips in 1 piece; 1 1/2 yards would be enough if strips are cut by fabric width)
- Backing 94" x 108"
- Batting 94" x 108"
- 11 yards self-made or purchased binding (if self-made, use remainder of matching print to make binding strips on lengthwise grain of fabric)

Figure 1 for color placement.

Step 5. Press all blocks and arrange in rows referring to the Placement Diagram for arrangement. Join blocks in rows; join rows to complete quilt center; press.

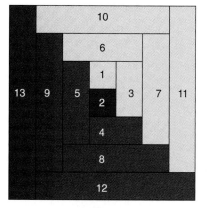

Figure 1
Piece blocks in numerical
order as shown.

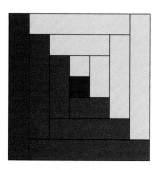

Log Cabin
14" x 14" Block
Make 42 blocks

Step 6. Cut two border strips on lengthwise grain of the print for top and bottom 3 1/2" x 84 1/2". Sew on and press. Cut two more strips 3 1/2" x 104 1/2"; sew to long sides; press.

Step 7. Finish quilt as desired referring to Pages 159–160 for instructions and choices.

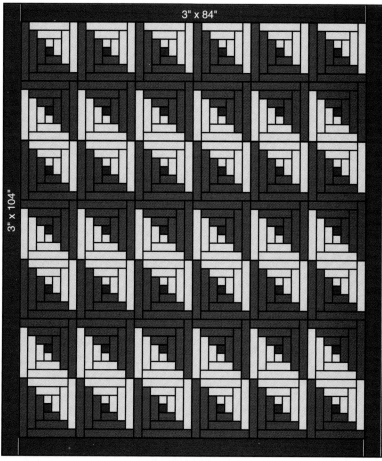

Log Cabin Quilt
Placement Diagram
90" x 104"

Log Cabin Gallery

This *Pepper Quilt,* so named because of its strong peppery smell, is an excellent example of the Log Cabin quilts which were so popular in Northeast Kansas over 100 years ago.

The late Winifred Campbell helped research the life of Myra Peters, whose name is precisely inked on a signature tag on the back of the quilt. Through Winifred and a former student of Miss Peters, quilt historians learned that she was an unmarried longtime school teacher who was born in 1861 and died in 1931. The student's sister Katherine, also unmarried, was her companion and housekeeper. Myra taught in Wetmore, Kan., from 1895–1930.

Although it was first thought that Myra made the quilt, the fabrics used in it date from a period before her birth to just after. Unless she stitched the quilt with old fabrics saved up by her ancestors, apparently Myra received it as a gift..

The quilt is called the *Pepper Quilt* because there has always been a whiff of black pepper when it is unfolded after being stored, causing everyone nearby to sneeze.

One of Myra Peters' pupils solved the riddle. Myra used black pepper as a deodorant. Whenever students got close to her, they would sneeze. She must have used the quilt on her bed and the pepper rubbed off her onto the quilt, where the smell has outlasted many of the fabrics as you can see by its fragile condition.

From Helen King

By Helen King

Round & Round the Log Cabin

This fascinating variation requires some very long strips for the outer logs. Although this is a very simple quilt design, it is easy to create a quilt with unequal sides unless you stop to check measurements often. It might help to draw out the rounds and figure out their correct size before sewing.

Begin the *Round & Round the Log Cabin* quilt in the center just as you would on a smaller block. Continue adding fabric strips around the center. With each addition, depending on the width of the strips, the strip gets longer. As construction proceeds, the strips become longer than the width of a normal piece of fabric.

When this happens, you may either cut lengthwise strips or sew two widths of fabric together to create longer strips which may be trimmed to size before sewing to the sides, or sewn to the sides and then trimmed after sewing.

If you choose to trim after sewing, be very careful that strips on both sides of the log remain the same size. If one side changes by even just 1/16" on every round, after 16 rounds one side of the quilt top is 1" larger than the other. This size discrepancy would be very noticeable on a large quilt.

Look closely at the photograph of the quilt shown. You will see that the bottom right corner has a break in the pattern where four strips ended the same length. A similar break in the pattern appears in the upper left corner. The pattern continues again after these breaks. These strange breaks in the design were added

Quilt Specifications
Skill Level: Easy　　**Quilt Size:** 96" x 112"

Materials
• 3 1/2 yards each light and dark print scraps • Backing 100" x 116" • Batting 100" x 116" • 11 1/2 yards self-made or purchased binding • All-purpose thread to match fabrics

to make the quilt a rectangle instead of a square. If you prefer, you could add these strips at the top and bottom edges as shown on the Placement Diagram.

The light/dark sides create a distinct diagonal design so if you want to add length to your finished square, add strips to the top and bottom.

If you like surprises and unexpected things to happen on your quilts—things that others will wonder about—you, too, can create some change of design that will confuse future owners of the quilt.

We always wonder why a quilt has some strange quirk. Sometimes it is intentional; sometimes it is not. Why not leave the reason a mystery? It is more fun that way.

Instructions

Step 1. Cut one 4 1/2" x 4 1/2" square dark fabric for center square.

Step 2. Cut remaining fabrics for shorter logs 2 1/2" by fabric width. Cut fabrics for longer logs in either lengthwise strips (if you have yardage this length) or cut two strips of each fabric to seam together to create longer strips.

Step 3. Sew a light strip to the center square as shown in Figure 1. Trim even; press.

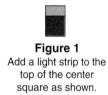

Figure 1
Add a light strip to the
top of the center
square as shown.

Step 4. Sew another light strip to the adjacent side of the center square as shown in Figure 2. Trim even; press.

Figure 2
Add a light strip to
the adjacent side.

Step 5. Sew a dark strip to the two remaining sides referring to Figure 3. Trim even; press.

Figure 3
Add dark strips to the
remaining 2 sides.

Step 6. Continue adding strips to sides, keeping two sides light and two sides dark, until the quilt is the desired width; press after each addition. It will be square if all stitching is accurate.

Step 7. Sew more strips to the top and bottom to add length to the quilt if a rectangle is desired as shown in the Placement Diagram.

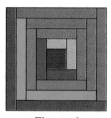

Figure 4
Continue adding light and
dark strips to the center to
create the design as shown.

Step 8. Finish quilt in chosen method referring to Pages 152–160 for instructions.

Tips & Techniques

If you really want to have fun, make the strips varied widths as shown in Figure 5. Piecing several light prints together to create one long strip would make a very scrappy quilt. It might not win a prize for design and composition, but it would be a fun quilt to construct, and it will use up scraps quickly. Sometimes we want a stress-free project; making this quilt with no rules is about as stress-free as it gets!

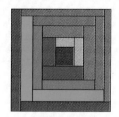

Figure 5
Adding strips of varied widths to the center
makes an unusual quilt, which could end
up with the center square not centered!

Round & Round the Log Cabin
Placement Diagram
96" x 112"

By Norma Compagna

Chimneys & Cornerstones

There is a real challenge in making traditional quilts in new and creative ways. The block unit used for this interesting design is similar to a Log Cabin block in that the block begins in the center and rows are added around it.

The center of the block unit used in the *Chimneys & Cornerstones* quilt shown is a Nine-Patch. Each subsequent round is added using a method similar to those given in the instruction section and specific instructions for piecing are given for this method.

As the rounds are added, a diagonal design takes form as the corner squares create the cornerstones and the strips form the chimneys as mentioned in the quilt's name.

More blocks may be added to create a larger quilt; remember to adjust the materials list accordingly.

Instructions

Step 1. Cut fabrics into 1 1/2" by fabric width strips as follows: fabric 1—cut 20 strips; fabric 2—cut 13 strips; fabric 3—cut 26 strips; and fabric 4—cut 38 strips.

Step 2. Sort strips into colors.

Step 3. Sew one strip set of each color set using fabrics 1 and 4 for Nine-Patch A Units as shown in Figure 1. Repeat for two strip sets of the 1-4-1 combination. Cut strips into 1 1/2" segments.

Step 4. Join the cut segments to create Nine-Patch A Units as shown in Figure 2. Complete 26 of these units for blocks and sashing.

Quilt Specifications

Skill Level: Intermediate **Quilt Size:** 45" x 59"
Block Size: 11" x 11"
Number of Blocks: 12

Materials

- 1 1/4 yards fabric 1 (lightest color)
- 1 1/4 yards fabric 2 (medium/light)
- 1 1/4 yards fabric 3 (medium/dark)
- 2 1/2 yards fabric 4 (dark)
- Backing 49" x 63"
- Batting 49" x 63"
- All-purpose thread to match fabrics
- 6 yards self-made or purchased binding

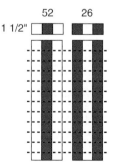

Figure 1
Sew fabrics 1 and 4 together as shown. Cut into 1 1/2" segments.

Figure 2
Sew 1 1/2" segments together as shown to make Nine-Patch A Units.

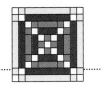

Step 5. Repeat with one strip set of each color set using fabrics 1 and 3 for Nine-Patch B Units as shown in Figure 3. Complete six Nine-Patch B Units for blocks.

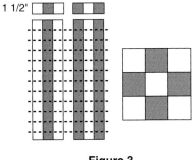

Figure 3
Sew fabrics 1 and 3 together as shown. Cut into 1 1/2" segments. Resew to make Nine-Patch B Units.

Step 6. Sew four strips each fabrics 3 and 4 together and cut into 3 1/2" segments as shown in Figure 4. You will need 48 segments to complete the quilt as shown.

Step 7. Sew four strips each fabrics 2 and 4 together and cut into 7 1/2" segments as shown in Figure 5. You will need 24 segments for Block B.

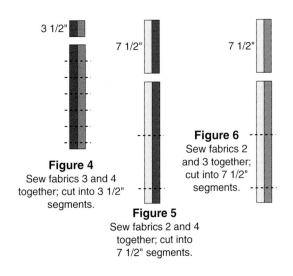

Figure 4
Sew fabrics 3 and 4 together; cut into 3 1/2" segments.

Figure 5
Sew fabrics 2 and 4 together; cut into 7 1/2" segments.

Figure 6
Sew fabrics 2 and 3 together; cut into 7 1/2" segments.

Step 8. Sew four strips each fabrics 2 and 3 together and cut into 7 1/2" segments as shown in Figure 6. You will need 24 segments for Block A.

Step 9. Sew two fabric 4 strips to one fabric 3 strip as shown in Figure 7. Cut into 11 1/2" segments. Repeat for 11 strip units. You will need 31 segments for sashing.

Step 10. Sew four strip sets fabrics 4 and 1 for Four-Patch A Units as shown in Figure 8. Cut into 1 1/2" segments. You will need 48 segments. Restitch to make 24 Four-Patch A Units. Repeat with fabrics 3 and 1 for 48 segments to make 24 Four-Patch B Units and with fabrics 2 and 1 for 96 segments for 48 Four-Patch C Units.

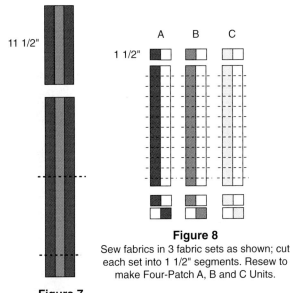

Figure 8
Sew fabrics in 3 fabric sets as shown; cut each set into 1 1/2" segments. Resew to make Four-Patch A, B and C Units.

Figure 7
Sew fabrics 3 and 4 together; cut into 11 1/2" segments.

Step 11. Arrange Four-Patch Units with Nine-Patch centers and sew together to make six A Blocks as shown in Figure 9.

Step 12. Arrange Four-Patch Units with Nine-Patch centers and sew together to make six B Blocks as shown in Figure 10.

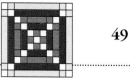
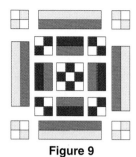

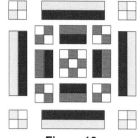

Figure 9
Arrange Four-Patch Units with Nine-Patch centers; sew to make A Blocks as shown.

Figure 10
Arrange Four-Patch Units with Nine-Patch centers; sew to make B Blocks as shown.

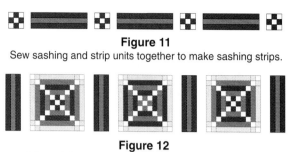

Figure 11
Sew sashing and strip units together to make sashing strips.

Figure 12
Join sashing strips and pieced blocks to make a row.

Step 13. Sew sashing Nine-Patch Units with sashing strips as shown in Figure 11; repeat for five strip units.

Step 14. Sew a sashing strip to a block to a strip to a block to a strip to a block to a strip as

shown in Figure 12; repeat for four rows.

Step 15. Arrange sashing-strip rows with block rows referring to the Placement Diagram; join in rows and press.

Step 16. Finish quilt in chosen method referring to Pages 159–160.

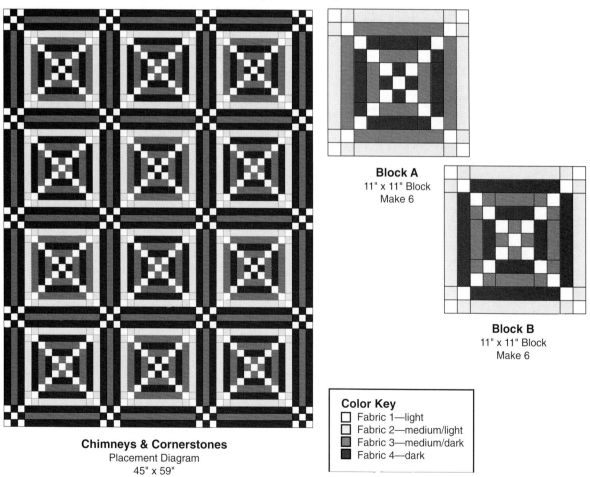

Chimneys & Cornerstones
Placement Diagram
45" x 59"

Block A
11" x 11" Block
Make 6

Block B
11" x 11" Block
Make 6

Color Key
☐ Fabric 1—light
☐ Fabric 2—medium/light
▨ Fabric 3—medium/dark
■ Fabric 4—dark

By LaRayne Meyer

Cutting Corners
Pineapple Block Variation

If you have already tried making a pineapple-type Log Cabin block, you know how difficult it can be. Try placing folded triangles at the corners of each round of a Log Cabin block to give an illusion of the pineapple design without all the work!

Using a dark plaid fabric in the center and dark-colored logs creates a masculine-looking quilt. Accenting the corners with black triangles produces a nice design with a warm look.

For fun, try substituting preprinted panels in the center or use up the pockets from old jeans to create a playful and sturdy quilt for children or teens.

If you don't like the pockets formed by the triangles on the corners being left open, machine- or hand-stitch across the folded edge to secure. The underneath layers may be trimmed away to reduce bulk.

Instructions

Step 1. Cut four strips plaid 6" by fabric width. Cut into 24 squares 6" x 6".

Step 2. Cut 24 strips black solid 3 3/4" by fabric width. Cut strips into 288 squares 3 3/4" x 3 3/4".

Step 3. Cut print fabrics in 2" by fabric width strips.

Step 4. Cut seven strips plaid 2 1/2" by width of fabric; set aside for border/binding.

Step 5. Choose any 2" strip and sew to one

Quilt Specifications	
Skill Level: Easy	**Quilt Size:** 61" x 90"
Block Size: 14 1/2" x 14 1/2"	
Number of Blocks: 24	

Materials
• 2 yards plaid for center squares and binding
• 1/2 yard each 6 coordinating prints
• 2 1/2 yards black solid
• Backing 62" x 91"
• Batting 62" x 91"
• 2 skeins black embroidery floss
• All-purpose thread to match fabrics

Figure 1
Sew a strip to 1 side of
the center square and
trim as shown.

side of the center square; press and trim even with square as shown in Figure 1. Add same-color strip to opposite side and trim as shown in Figure 2. Continue to add strips until center square has one strip on each side as shown in Figure 3.

 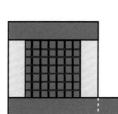

Figure 2
Sew the same color strip to the opposite side of the center square and trim as shown.

Figure 3
Add the next strip to opposite sides as before.

Step 6. Fold four black triangles in half on the diagonal. Place triangle on the previously pieced unit with corners even; machine-baste or pin to hold in place.

Folded edge (open underneath)

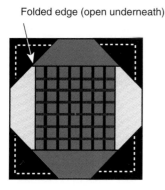

Figure 4
Fold triangle and place corners even with edge of pieced section; machine-baste in place.

Step 7. Add another round of logs to each side of stitched center as in Step 5, pressing and trimming after each addition. Add folded black triangles to corners as in Step 6.

Step 8. Continue adding strips and folded triangles to complete the block. Repeat for 24 blocks.

Step 9. Arrange the blocks in six rows of four blocks each. Join the blocks in rows; press. Join the rows to complete the top; press.

Step 10. Sandwich batting between completed top and prepared backing piece. Safety-pin or baste layers together to hold flat.

Step 11. Using 6 strands of embroidery floss, tack the quilt layers together using a square knot (see Page 156). Knots may be placed at the center of each block and at the corners where blocks join, or as desired.

Step 12. When tying is complete, trim edges 1" larger than quilt top all around.

Step 13. Join the 2 1/2" strips cut in Step 4 at short ends to make one long strip. Sew to sides at fabric edge, not at backing and binding edge, folding to miter at corners. *Note: This excess allows the binding edge to serve as a border and binding at the same time. Miter corners referring to Pages 152–153 for instructions.*

Step 14. Turn under edges of outside edge of border 1/4". Turn to the back and hand-stitch in place to finish. *Note: Border strip should finish at 1 1/2" on front edge of quilt.*

Tips & Techniques

If you prefer all blocks to be made in the same color sequence, remember to purchase more fabric for outer strips than for inner strips. Using random placement requires no planning, and making mistakes in color placement is eliminated. As you piece the blocks you will develop your own methods of speed-piecing to save time. Remember that you can add borders or increase or decrease the number of blocks to change the size of the completed quilt.

Cutting Corners Pineapple
14 1/2" x 14 1/2" Block

Cutting Corners Pineapple
Placement Diagram
61" x 90"

By Nancy Kiman

Round-About
Log Cabin Medallion

Combine narrow and wide strips to make the Log Cabin blocks in the center of this medallion quilt. Add a large floral print with coordinating solids and a stripe and the resulting quilt looks and feels warm and cozy.

When you combine narrow logs on one side of the Log Cabin block with wider strips on the other side, you get an off-center log. Using the same fabrics in each log on each side creates a very different effect.

The quilt shown is a medallion style that uses only 16 blocks in the center. A stripe border surrounds the center with large triangles to square it off. Wider borders on the top and bottom elongate the quilt from a square to a rectangle so that it will fit a bed with the Log Cabin design in the center.

This quilt was machine-quilted in a meandering pattern in the large triangles and border strips, making it a quick and easy project.

Quilt Specifications

Skill Level: Easy　**Quilt Size:** 63" x 85"
Block Size: 5 1/2" x 5 1/2"
Number of Blocks: 16

Materials

- 1/2 yard cream solid
- 2 3/4 yards small floral print
- 2 1/4 yards coordinating stripe
- 3/4 yard large floral print
- 1 1/4 yards mauve solid
- Backing 67" x 89"
- Batting 67" x 89"
- All-purpose thread to match fabrics
- 8 1/2 yards self-made or purchased binding

Instructions

Step 1. Cut 10 strips cream solid 1" by fabric width. Cut one strip 1 1/2" by fabric width.

Step 2. Cut 10 strips small floral print 1 1/2" by fabric width.

Step 3. Sew a 1 1/2" cream solid strip to a 1 1/2" floral print strip; press seam to print side.

Step 4. Cut sewn strip into 1 1/2" segments; you will need 16 segments. Set aside remaining piece of strip for another project.

Step 5. Sew the pieced segment to a cream strip. Continue adding segments to the strip until all segments are used. Press and trim strip even with segments.

Step 6. Sew the pieced segment to a floral print strip, referring to Figure 1 for placement. Sew and cut as before as shown in Figure 2. Continue adding strips until you have three narrow strips on one side

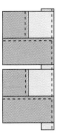

Figure 1
Sew the pieced segments to the cream solid strip.

of the pieced center and three wide strips on the opposite side referring to Figure 3 for order of placement. Note that the pieced segment is not in the center of the block.

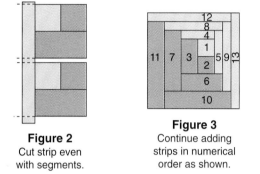

Figure 2
Cut strip even with segments.

Figure 3
Continue adding strips in numerical order as shown.

Step 7. Complete 16 blocks; press and square up to 6" x 6" if necessary.

Step 8. Arrange four blocks in two rows as shown in Figure 4. Make a four-block section. Repeat for four sections. Join the sections to complete the center referring to Figure 5.

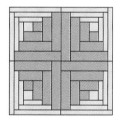

Figure 4
Arrange 4 blocks as shown.

Figure 5
Sew the 4-block units together for center as shown.

Step 9. Press and square up center section to 22 1/2" x 22 1/2" if necessary.

Step 10. Cut four strips stripe fabric 3" x 27 1/2". Sew a strip to each side of the center, mitering corners; press seams toward border.

Step 11. Cut two squares large floral print 20" x 20". Cut each square on the diagonal once to make two triangles. Sew a triangle to each side of the pieced center. Press seams toward the triangle. Square up pieced center to 38 1/2" x 38 1/2", if necessary.

Step 12. Cut two strips mauve solid 2" x 38 1/2". Sew a strip to opposite sides of the pieced center. Cut two more strips 2" x 41 1/2"; sew to top and bottom. Press seams toward the strips.

Step 13. Cut two strips large floral print 6 1/2" x 41 1/2". Sew a strip to two opposite sides of the quilt center. Cut two more strips 12 1/2" x 53 1/2". Sew to the top and bottom of the quilt center. Press seams toward border strips.

Step 14. Cut two strips cream solid 5 1/2" x 53 1/2". Sew to top and bottom of quilt center; press seams toward border strips.

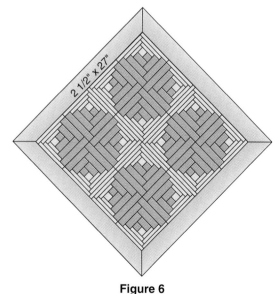

Figure 6
Sew border strips to quilt center as shown; finished size given.

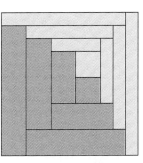

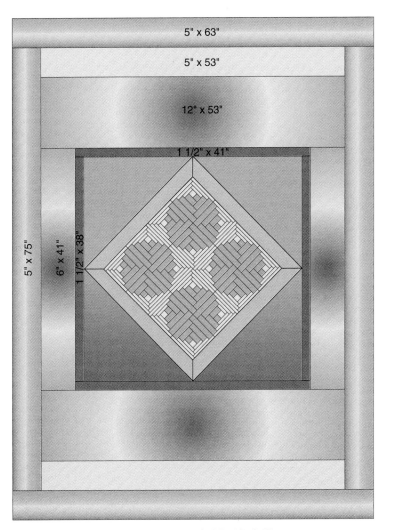

Round-About Log Cabin Medallion
Placement Diagram
63" x 85"

Off-Center Log Cabin
5 1/2" x 5 1/2" Block

Step 15. Cut two strips stripe 5 1/2" x 75 1/2"; sew to long sides of quilt center. Cut two more strips 5 1/2" x 63 1/2"; sew to top and bottom of quilt center. Press seams toward border strips.

Step 16. Mark the top for quilting, if necessary. The quilt shown is machine-quilted on the diagonal in each Log Cabin block, in the ditch of all border strips and meander-quilted in the large triangles and the wide border strips.

Step 17. Sandwich batting between completed top and prepared backing piece. Safety-pin or baste layers together to hold flat.

Step 18. Quilt on marked lines and as desired. When quilting is complete, trim edges even and remove basting or pins.

Step 19. Finish edges with self-made or purchased binding referring to Page 157 for instructions.

Tips & Techniques

When using stripes in borders, remember to cut the strips on the lengthwise grain of the fabric. This will mean that more yardage will be needed because of the length needed for the border strips. The leftover fabrics can be used for other coordinating projects to place in the room your quilt calls home, or pieced with other leftover fabrics to create a coordinating backing for the quilt.

By Joyce Mori

Log Cabin Color Blocks

*There seem to be endless varieties, and the choice of fabrics and
the placement of color makes each one unique. I have a large fabric stash,
and every so often I decide it is time to use up small pieces of fabric in my collection.
This Log Cabin design is perfect for that. The bright colors of this scrap
quilt are also perfect if you wish to make a quilt for a child.*

The method of construction for these blocks is a bit different due to the experimentation with colors.

Begin by making copies of the line drawing for this quilt in Figure 1. The line drawing is done in triangles rather than pieced Log Cabin blocks. The triangle drawing allows you to see how you can color in squares of color. If you

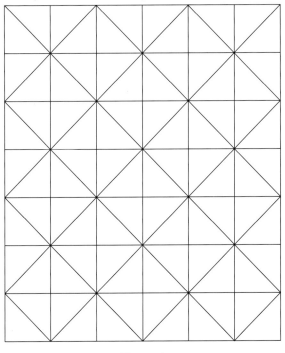

Figure 1
Copy the drawing as shown; color triangles to make design.

Quilt Specifications

Skill Level: Easy   **Quilt Size:** 57" x 66 1/2"
Block Size: 9 1/2" x 9 1/2"
Number of Blocks: 42

Materials

- 1/3 yard red solid
- Scraps or fat quarters of the following color fabrics: light and dark blue; light and dark purple; light and dark red; light, medium and dark green; light and medium gray; black; yellow; orange; and peach
- Backing 61" x 70"
- Batting 61" x 70"
- All-purpose thread to match fabrics
- 7 1/2 yards self-made or purchased binding

look at a block you can see that it is divided in half with a different color in each half. One half of the square has a dark color and the other half a light color. Placement of the colors is arbitrary; do what you find pleasing.

If you color in the line drawing first, you will have a plan for sewing the blocks. You can make some squares more prominent by using some very dark fabrics or you can make the squares fade in and out by using some medium fabrics.

The squares in my quilt do not always stand out because I used some medium-value fabrics. If you want a more planned formal look, position the dark squares carefully and use dark fabrics along the outside edges. The center square in this quilt block is always red and provides a constant in the design.

This pattern is a variation of the Sunshine and Shadows design; however, in the traditional coloring of the design the center squares are colored so they are very distinct.

Instructions

Step 1. Cut three strips red solid 2 1/2" by fabric width; cut each strip into 2 1/2" segments. You will need 42 segments for centers.

Step 2. Sort through your fabrics. Rotary-cut a wide selection of light and dark strips 1 3/4" wide in a wide range of your fabrics.

Step 3. Referring to Figure 1, color triangles in your selected fabric colors. The triangles reflect

Figure 2
The quilt shown in the photo and Placement Diagram looks like this when Figure 1 is colored in.

half of a Log Cabin block. Figure 2 shows the color arrangement used for the quilt shown. Figure 5 shows how many blocks of each color are needed to make the quilt as shown. If you change colors, use these drawings as guides to create the number of blocks needed to complete the quilt as you have drawn it.

Step 4. To construct blocks, begin in the center with a 2 1/2" red segment. Add the first two logs to the center square as shown in Figure 3 referring to Figure 5 for color arrangement of each type of block or to your own drawings for your color version.

Step 5. Continue adding logs 3 and 4 referring to Figure 4. Complete all of one block combination color block before starting another color. For example, make two yellow/green blocks before starting the two yellow/blue blocks.

Figure 3
Sew rounds 1 and 2 to the center square.

Figure 4
Continue adding rounds 3 and 4.

Step 6. As you sew, iron the seam allowance under and trim off the strip even with the previous segment.

Step 7. Check off the blocks as you complete them in Figure 5 or in your own drawings.

Step 8. Complete 42 blocks; press and square blocks to 10" x 10".

Step 9. Arrange blocks in six rows of seven blocks each referring to the Placement Diagram.

Step 10. Sandwich batting between completed top and prepared backing piece. Safety-pin or baste layers together to hold flat.

Step 11. Finish quilt in chosen method referring to Pages 152–160.

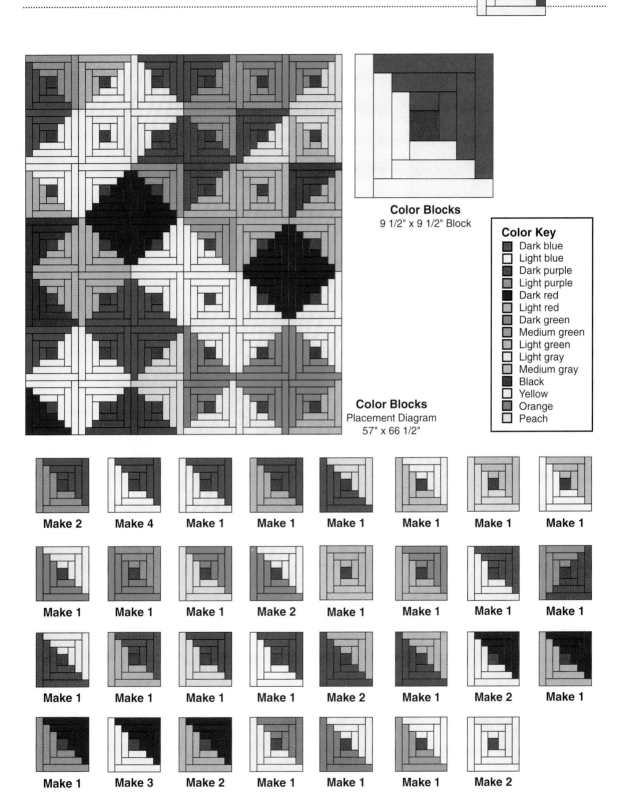

Color Blocks
9 1/2" x 9 1/2" Block

Color Blocks
Placement Diagram
57" x 66 1/2"

Color Key
- Dark blue
- Light blue
- Dark purple
- Light purple
- Dark red
- Light red
- Dark green
- Medium green
- Light green
- Light gray
- Medium gray
- Black
- Yellow
- Orange
- Peach

Make 2 Make 4 Make 1 Make 1 Make 1 Make 1 Make 1 Make 1

Make 1 Make 1 Make 1 Make 2 Make 1 Make 1 Make 1 Make 1

Make 1 Make 1 Make 1 Make 1 Make 2 Make 1 Make 2 Make 1

Make 1 Make 3 Make 2 Make 1 Make 1 Make 1 Make 2

Figure 5
Complete blocks in colors and numbers shown to make quilt shown in the photo and Placement Diagram.

By Chris Carlson

Antique Fabric
Half-Blocks

If you like to collect antique or vintage fabrics, this little half-block Log Cabin quilt allows you to use tiny scraps to create the logs. Remember to sign and date your finished quilt to prevent someone 100 years from now from thinking the quilt was made in the 1800s!

The versatile Log Cabin block can take on many faces. In this small quilt, logs are added to only one side of the square to create a half-block.

To unify the design, the square and the second round of logs are the same fabric, although each block is different. Pink-on-pink print is used for the last round of logs of each block, which really ties the blocks together.

Be on the lookout for antique fabrics at yard sales or flea markets. Don't worry about the sizes of the patches because the blocks in this quilt use tiny strips. If you want to copy the quilters from the time period of the fabrics used in this quilt, smaller pieces may be stitched together to make a piece large enough to use.

Cutting Instructions

Step 1. Stack the 12 assorted light print fabrics and cut from each piece as follows: one square 2" x 2" for piece A; one strip 1" x 2 1/2" for piece D; and one strip 1" x 3" for piece E.

Step 2. Stack the 12 assorted dark print fabrics and cut from each piece: one strip 1" x 2" for piece B and one strip 1" x 2 1/2" for piece C.

Step 3. Cut the following from pink print: 12 strips each 1" x 3" for piece F and 12 strips

Quilt Specifications

Skill Level: Easy   **Quilt Size:** 12" x 15 1/2"
Block Size: 3" x 3"   **Number of Blocks:** 12

Materials

- 5" x 6" piece each of 12 assorted light print fabrics
- 4" x 4 1/2" piece each of 12 assorted dark print fabrics
- 9" x 14" piece of pink print
- 9" x 12 1/2" piece of pink-and-black check for sashing
- 8" x 20" piece dark blue print for border
- Backing 15" x 18"
- Batting 15" x 18"
- All-purpose thread to match fabrics
- 6" x 20" fabric piece for binding

each 1" x 3 1/2" for piece G.

Step 4. From pink-and-black check, cut eight strips 1" x 3 1/2" for piece H and three strips 1" x 10 1/2" for piece I.

Step 5. From dark blue print cut two strips 1" x 10 1/2" for border piece J and two strips 1 1/2" x 16" for border piece K.

Step 6. From binding fabric, cut two strips 1" x 12 1/2" and two strips 1" x 18".

Piecing Instructions

Step 1. Sew a 1" x 2" dark strip to the left side of a 2" light square as shown in Figure 1; press. Sew a matching 1" x 2 1/2" dark strip to the top of the piece; press.

Figure 1
Sew a 1" x 2" dark
strip to the left side of
the light square.

Step 2. Sew a 1" x 2 1/2" light strip to the left side of the piece. Sew a matching 1" x 3" light strip to the top of the piece; press.

Step 3. Sew a 1" x 3" pink print strip to the left of the piece; sew a matching 1" x 3 1/2" pink print strip to the top of the piece to complete one block as shown in Figure 2; press. Repeat for 12 blocks.

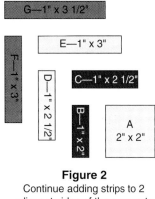

Figure 2
Continue adding strips to 2
adjacent sides of the square to
complete the block as shown.

Step 4. Press blocks on both sides; square up to 3 1/2" x 3 1/2" if necessary.

Step 5. Arrange the blocks in four rows of three blocks each.

Step 6. Sew two H pink-and-black check sashing strips, each 1" x 3 1/2", between three blocks to make one row as shown in Figure 3. Repeat for four rows; press.

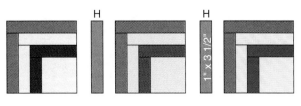

Figure 3
Sew 3 blocks together with 2 H 1" x 3 1/2" sashing strips. Press seams toward strips as shown.

Step 7. Sew three I pink-and-black check sashing strips each 1" x 10 1/2" between the four rows to complete quilt center as shown in Figure 4; press.

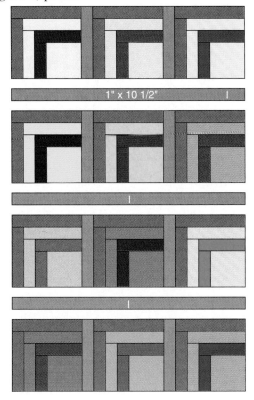

Figure 4
Join the 4 rows with 3 I 1" x 10 1/2" sashing strips as shown.

Step 8. Sew a 1 1/2" x 10 1/2" dark blue J border strip to the top and bottom of the quilt center; press seams toward the border strips.

Step 9. Sew a 1 1/2" x 16" dark blue K border strip to the sides of the quilt center; press seams toward the border strips.

Antique Half-Block
3" x 3" Block

Antique Half-Block Miniature
Placement Diagram
12" x 15 1/2"

Finishing

Step 1. Mark the top for quilting, if necessary. The quilt shown was quilted in the center of every strip and diagonally from corner to corner in the squares.

Step 2. Sandwich batting between completed top and prepared backing piece. Safety-pin or baste layers together to hold flat.

Step 3. Quilt on marked lines and as desired. When quilting is complete, trim edges even and remove basting or pins.

Step 4. Cut the 6" x 20" binding fabric into two

1" x 12 1/2" and two 1" x 18" strips. Sew a shorter strip to opposite sides of the quilt center, extending the strip an equal amount on both ends. Trim excess even with quilt top as shown in Figure 5. Fold over raw edge 1/4" and turn to backside; hand-stitch in place.

Step 5. Sew longer strips to the remaining two sides as in Step 4. Trim ends to extend 3/8" beyond end of quilt edge. Fold ends under as shown in Figure 6. Turn to back and hand-stitch in place to finish.

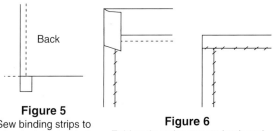

Figure 5
Sew binding strips to opposite sides of quilt center; trim ends even.

Figure 6
Fold ends under, turn to back and hand-stitch in place as shown.

By Chris Carlson

Miniature Log House

Houses are very appealing in miniature and even more so when finished with a log frame. Such a frame on a house block makes it a true Log Cabin House pattern. This delightful pattern is broken down into four easy-to-assemble units. The many fabrics in the quilt make it fun to sew and fun to own, and the bright colors help to make the small, individual pieces noticeable.

If you prefer to hand-piece the small blocks in this quilt, use the full-size drawing given in Figure 1 to create templates referring to Page 145 for instructions. The full-size pattern may also be used as a paper-piecing foundation if you make the block in sections. Figure 1 separates the sections with lines to indicate these sections.

The instructions given here are for fast-cutting and piecing techniques using small pieces of fabric. Although they seem long and complicated, they are easy. It takes longer to read the instructions than it does to follow them!

Have fun with this house design in whatever method you choose to use to make it.

Cutting Instructions

Step 1. Cut the following from light blue print: one strip 1 1/4" x 15" for sky piece A; one strip 1" x 8" for sky piece B; one strip 1 1/4" x 9" for sky piece C; and one strip 1 5/8" x 11" for sky piece D.

Step 2. Cut one strip black print 3/4" x 8" for chimney piece E.

Step 3. Cut two strips brown print 1 1/4" x 15" for roof piece F.

Quilt Specifications
Skill Level: Intermediate
Quilt Size: 13" x 17 1/2"
Block Size: 4 1/2" x 4 1/2"
Number of Blocks: 6

Materials
• 8" x 17" piece light blue print for sky
• 2" x 10" piece black print for chimney
• 4" x 17" piece brown print for roof
• 6" x 11" piece red-and-white print for house front
• 3" x 11" piece medium blue print for door
• 3" x 10" piece yellow print for window
• 6" x 12" piece green print for grass
• 4" x 14" piece pink print for walkway
• 7" x 10" piece purple print for logs
• 7" x 11" piece pink-and-blue print for logs
• 7" x 12" piece dark blue print for logs
• 7" x 14" piece yellow-and-pink print for logs
• 12" x 16" piece red check for border
• Backing 16" x 21"
• Batting 16" x 21"
• All-purpose thread to match fabrics
• 6" x 20" piece blue-and-white plaid for binding

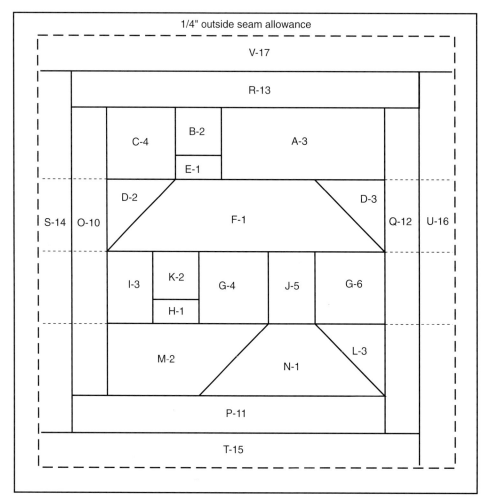

Figure 1
Use this full-size drawing as a pattern to create templates or to make paper-piecing foundations. The marks on each side show where the block must be cut apart to created paper-pieced sections which can be resewn after piecing. Piece in numerical order in each section. ***Note:*** *Pattern is reversed for paper piecing.*

Step 4. Cut the following from red-and-white print: two strips 1 1/4" x 9" for house front G; one strip 3/4" x 8" for house front H; and one strip 1" x 9" for house front I.

Step 5. Cut one strip medium blue print 1" x 9" for door piece J. Cut one strip yellow print 1" x 8" for window K.

Step 6. Cut the following from green print: one strip 1 5/8" x 6" for grass L and two strips 1 1/4" x 10" for grass M.

Step 7. Cut two strips pink print 1 1/4" x 12" for walkway piece N.

Step 8. Cut six strips purple print 7/8" x 3 1/2" for log O and six strips 7/8" x 3 7/8" for log P.

Step 9. Cut six strips pink-and-blue print 7/8" x 3 7/8" for log Q and six strips 7/8" x 4 1/4" for log R.

Step 10. Cut six strips dark blue print 7/8" x 4 1/4" for log S and six strips 7/8" x 4 5/8" for log T.

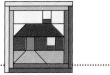
Step 11. Cut six strips yellow-and-pink print 7/8" x 4 5/8" for log U and six strips 7/8" x 5" for log V.

Step 12. Cut two strips red check 2 1/2" x 14" and two strips 2 1/2" x 13 1/2" for borders.

Step 13. Cut two strips from the 6" x 20" blue-and-white plaid 1" x 18" and two strips 1" x 15 1/2" for binding.

Piecing Instructions

Note: Press all seams open and trim seams to 1/8" unless otherwise indicated. Arrows on drawings indicate pressing direction.

Step 1. Sew a 1" x 8" light blue strip to a 3/4" x 8" black strip. Cut six 1" segments from the strips for B-E.

Step 2. Cut six 2 1/4" segments from a 1 1/4" x 15" light blue strip for A. Sew one of these segments to one segment made in Step 1 to make one B-E-A set as shown in Figure 2; repeat to make six sets.

Step 3. Cut a 1 1/4" x 9" light blue strip into six 1 1/4" C segments. Sew a C segment to a B-E-A set to complete one B-E-A-C chimney unit as shown in Figure 3.

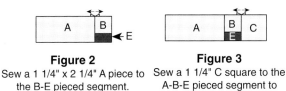

Figure 2
Sew a 1 1/4" x 2 1/4" A piece to the B-E pieced segment.

Figure 3
Sew a 1 1/4" C square to the A-B-E pieced segment to make chimney unit.

Step 4. Cut a 1 5/8" x 11" light blue print strip into six 1 5/8" squares. Stack these squares and cut in half once diagonally to make 12 D triangles.

Step 5. Stack two 1 1/4" x 15" brown strips; cut each strip into three 4 1/4" segments for a total of six segments. Stack these segments; cut one

45-degree angle off each side as shown in Figure 4 for F; set aside triangles.

Step 6. Sew a D triangle cut in Step 4 to each side of a piece cut in Step 5 to complete a D-F-D roof unit as shown in Figure 5; repeat to complete six units.

Figure 4
Cut pieces at a 45-degree angle on corners for F.

Figure 5
Complete the roof unit as shown.

Step 7. Sew a roof unit to a chimney unit as shown in Figure 6.

Step 8. Sew a 1 1/4" x 9" red-and-white strip to each side of a 1" x 9" medium blue strip. Cut six 1 1/4" segments from the pieced strips for G-J-G.

Step 9. Sew a 1" x 8" yellow strip to a 3/4" x 8" red-and-white strip. Cut six 1" segments from the pieced strips for K-H. Sew a K-H segment to a G-J-G segment; repeat for six K-H-G-J-G units.

Step 10. Cut six 1 1/4" segments from a 1" x 9" red-and-white strip for I. Sew one I segment to a K-H-G-J-G segment made in Step 9 to complete one house front unit as shown in Figure 7; repeat to complete six units.

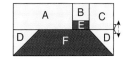

Figure 6
Sew a roof unit to a chimney unit.

Figure 7
Join units to complete a house front unit.

Step 11. Sew a house front unit to one chimney/roof unit as shown in Figure 8. Repeat for six units.

Step 12. Cut three 1 5/8" squares from a 1 5/8" x 6" green strip. Stack these squares; cut in half once on the diagonal to make six L triangles.

Figure 8
Join chimney/roof unit
with house front unit.

Step 13. Stack two 1 1/4" x 12" pink strips; cut three segments from each strip 3 1/4" to make six segments. Stack and cut these pieces on each side at a 45-degree angle for N; set aside triangles.

Step 14. Sew an L triangle to the left side of one N piece to make one set; repeat for six L-N sets.

Step 15. Stack the two 1 1/4" x 10" green strips; cut three 2 5/8" segments from each strip to make six segments. Stack right side up; cut a 45-degree angle off at the left sides from M; set aside triangles.

Step 16. Sew the M segments to the L-N segments to complete one walkway unit; repeat for six L-N-M units as shown in Figure 9.

Step 17. Sew a walkway unit to a chimney/ roof/house unit, matching door and walkway seams, to complete one house unit referring to Figure 10; repeat for six units.

Figure 9
Join pieces to make
walkway unit as shown.

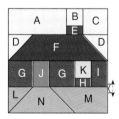

Figure 10
Sew a walkway unit to a
house/roof/chimney unit to
complete 1 house unit as shown.

Step 18. Press house units on both sides; square up to 3 1/2" x 3 1/2" if necessary.

Step 19. Sew a 7/8" x 3 1/2" purple O log strip

to the right side of each house unit. Repeat with the 7/8" x 3 7/8" purple P log strips on the bottom edge of each house unit referring to Figure 11.

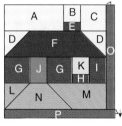

Figure 11
Sew log strips O and P to
house unit as shown.

Step 20. Sew a 7/8" x 3 7/8" blue-and-pink Q log strip to the left side of each house unit. Repeat with the 7/8" x 4 1/4" blue-and-pink R log strips to the top edge of each house unit.

Step 21. Sew a 7/8" x 4 1/4" dark blue S log strip to the right side of each house unit. Repeat with the 7/8" x 4 5/8" dark blue T strips on the bottom edge of each house unit.

Step 22. Sew a 7/8" x 4 5/8" yellow-and-pink U log strip to the left side of each house unit. Repeat with the 7/8" x 5" yellow-and-pink V log strips on the top edge of each house unit to complete six Miniature Log House blocks as shown in Figure 12.

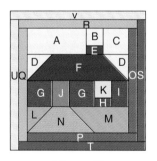

Figure 12
Continue adding log strips to house
unit in alphabetical order as shown.

Step 23. Press all blocks on both sides; square up to 5" x 5", if necessary.

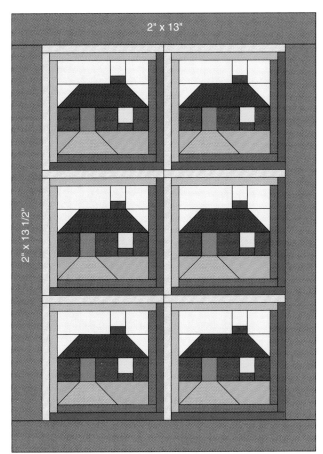

Miniature Log House
Placement Diagram
13" x 17 1/2"

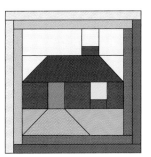

Miniature Log House
4 1/2" x 4 1/2" Block

Quilt Assembly

Step 1. Sew the blocks together in three rows of two blocks each, matching seams.

Step 2. Sew the 2 1/2" x 14" red check strips to the long sides of the pieced center; press seams toward border strips. Sew the 2 1/2" x 13 1/2" red check strips to the top and bottom; press seams toward border strips.

Step 3. Press the quilt top on both sides; check for proper seam pressing and trim all loose threads.

Step 4. Mark the top for quilting, if necessary. The quilt shown was quilted in the ditch of all seams.

Step 5. Sandwich batting between completed top and prepared backing piece. Safety-pin or baste layers together to hold flat.

Step 6. Quilt on marked lines and as desired. When quilting is complete, trim edges even and remove basting or pins.

Step 7. Sew a 1" x 18" binding strip to opposite long sides of the quilt center, extending the strip an equal amount on both ends. Trim excess even with quilt top, referring to Figure 13. Fold over raw edge 1/4" and turn to backside; hand-stitch in place.

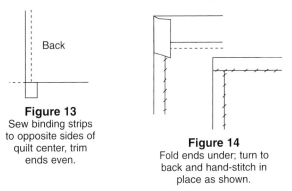

Figure 13
Sew binding strips to opposite sides of quilt center, trim ends even.

Figure 14
Fold ends under; turn to back and hand-stitch in place as shown.

Step 8. Sew the 1" x 15 1/2" strips to the top and bottom as in Step 7. Trim ends to extend 3/8" beyond end of quilt edge. Fold ends under as shown in Figure 14. Turn to back and hand-stitch in place to finish.

By Chris Carlson

Ohio Star Miniature

For this pattern, the star points are made with a quick and very accurate strip-piecing method, then the blocks are encircled with easy-to-sew log strips. Two rows of logs surround the pieced block in a Courthouse Steps fashion. Try this method with more strips or vary the size of the center blocks. This is a wonderful way to create a unique frame for pieced or appliquéd blocks while using the frame to create a secondary design.

Create templates from the full-size drawing of the Ohio Star block in Figure 13 or use fast-cutting and piecing methods as instructed. Tiny scraps of fabric can be used to make all blocks different, or purchased fabrics in a planned color arrangement could be used.

Making miniature quilts is the perfect way to try out a new method or pattern. If you really like the way it all goes together, you might like to try making the quilt on a larger scale.

Most miniature enthusiasts can't stop making miniatures. The high they get from finishing a project in several days instead of weeks, months or even years, can't be replaced. Once they are hooked, it seems larger quilts are too much trouble. Miniature quilts fit into the smallest areas and make wonderful gifts.

If you have ever tried to keep warm under one, you realize then that there are times when large quilts are important, too.

Cutting Instructions

Note: *A 1/4" seam allowance is included in all measurements.*

Step 1. Cut the following: eight strips 1 1/2" x 11" from red solid for A; four strips 1 1/2" x 11" light print for B; four strips 1 1/2" x 11" medi-

Quilt Specifications
Skill Level: Intermediate
Quilt Size: 13 1/2" x 18 1/2"
Block Size: 5" x 5"
Number of Blocks: 6

Materials
• 14" x 14" piece red solid
• 8" x 14" piece light print
• 8" x 14" piece medium blue print
• 8" x 14" piece medium pink print
• 13" x 16" piece dark blue solid
• 13" x 16" piece blue-and-white print
• 11" x 18" piece multi-floral for border
• Backing 16" x 21"
• Batting 16" x 21"
• All-purpose thread to match fabrics
• 6" x 21" piece pink solid for binding

um blue print for C; and four strips 1 1/2" x 11" medium pink print for D.

Step 2. From dark blue solid cut the following: one strip 1 1/2" x 11" for E; six strips 1" x 3 1/2" for F; six strips 1" x 4 1/2" for G; six strips 1" x 4 1/2" for L; and six strips 1" x 5 1/2" for M.

Step 3. From the blue-and-white print cut the following: six strips 1" x 3 1/2" for J; six strips 1" x 4 1/2" for H; six strips 1" x 4 1/2" for K; and six strips 1" x 5 1/2" for I.

Step 4. From the multi-floral print cut the following: two strips 2 1/4" x 15 1/2" and two strips 2 1/4" x 14" for borders.

Step 5. From the pink solid, cut the following: two strips 1" x 19" and two strips 1" x 16" for top and bottom binding.

Piecing Instructions

Note: *Press all seams open and trim to 1/8" unless otherwise directed.*

Step 1. Sew a red strip to a light print strip to make one set; repeat to make four sets. Cut six pieced 1 1/2" segments from each set for a total of 24 A-B segments referring to Figure 1.

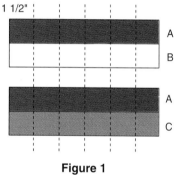

Figure 1
Sew 2 different strip sets as shown. Cut apart in 1 1/2" segments for A-B and A-C.

Step 2. Sew a red strip and a medium blue print strip to make one set; repeat to make four sets. From each set, cut six pieced 1 1/2" segments for a total of 24 A-C segments.

Step 3. Sew a red/light print A-B segment to a red/medium blue print A-C segment, matching center seams, to make a Four-Patch unit as shown in Figure 2. Repeat for 24 A-C-A-B units.

Step 4. Cut a 1 1/2" x 1 1/2" square from each

Four-Patch A-C-A-B unit using the seams as a cutting guide for a total of 24 squares as shown in Figure 3.

Figure 2
Sew A-C and A-B segments together to make a Four-Patch unit.

Figure 3
Cut 1 1/2" squares from each Four-Patch unit.

Step 5. Stack the four 1 1/2" x 11" pink print strips; cut six 1 1/2" x 1 1/2" segments from each strip for a total of 24 D squares.

Step 6. Sew a pink D square to opposite sides of one A-C-A-B unit to make one row unit referring to Figure 4; repeat for 12 D-A-C-A-B-D units.

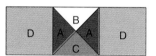

Figure 4
Sew a pink D square to each side of the A-C-A-B unit.

Step 7. Cut six 1 1/2" x 1 1/2" square segments from the 1 1/2" x 11" dark blue solid strip for E. Sew an A-C-A-B unit to opposite sides of a dark blue E square to make one row unit as shown in Figure 5; repeat for six units.

Figure 5
Sew an A-C-A-B unit to each side of a blue solid E square.

Step 8. Sew two D-A-C-A-B-D row units to the top and bottom of one A-C-A-B-E row unit, matching seams, to complete one Ohio Star block as shown in Figure 6. Repeat to make six blocks.

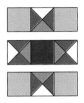

Figure 6
Join pieced rows to form
1 Ohio Star block.

Step 9. Press blocks on both sides; square up to 3 1/2" x 3 1/2" if necessary.

Step 10. Sew a 1" x 3 1/2" dark blue solid F strip to the left and right sides of three blocks. Sew a 1" x 4 1/2" dark blue solid G strip to the top and bottom of the same three blocks referring to Figure 7.

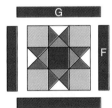

Figure 7
Sew dark blue F and G strips
to the sides and top and
bottom of the pieced block.

Step 11. Sew a 1" x 4 1/2" blue-and-white H strip to the left and right sides of the same three

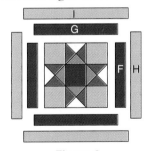

Figure 8
Sew blue-and-white print H and I
strips to the sides and top and
bottom of the pieced block to
complete Ohio Star A blocks.

blocks. Sew a 1" x 5 1/2" blue-and-white print I strip to the top and bottom of the same three blocks to complete three Ohio Star A blocks as shown in Figure 8.

Step 12. Sew a 1" x 3 1/2" blue-and-white print J strip to the top and bottom edges of the remaining three blocks. Sew a 1" x 4 1/2" blue-and-white print K strip to the left and right sides of the three blocks.

Step 13. Sew a 1" x 4 1/2" dark blue solid L strip to the top and bottom of the three blocks. Sew a 1" x 5 1/2" dark blue solid M strip to the left and right sides of the three blocks to complete three Ohio Star B blocks as shown in Figure 9.

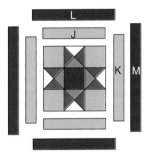

Figure 9
For Ohio Star B blocks, sew
blue-and-white J and K strips on pieced
block first. Add dark blue L and M strips
to complete Ohio Star B blocks.

Step 14. Press all blocks; square up to 5 1/2" if necessary.

Assembly

Step 1. Arrange the A and B blocks in three rows referring to Figure 10. Join in rows; join the rows to complete the pieced center. Press the seams all in one direction.

Step 2. Sew a 2 1/4" x 15 1/2" multi-floral border strip to the long sides of the quilt center; press seams toward borders. Sew the 2 1/4" x 14" border strips to the top and bottom; press seams toward border strips.

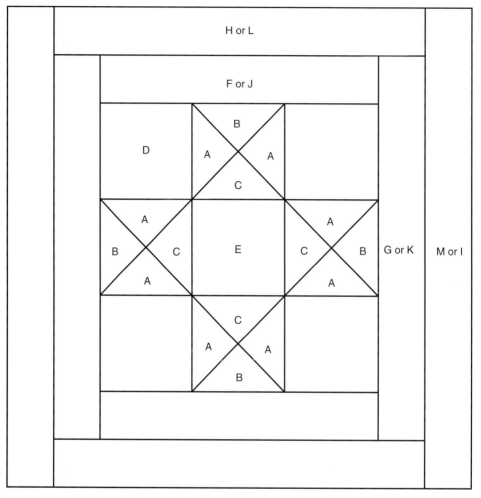

Figure 13
Make templates for hand-piecing from this full-size block drawing for Blocks A and B.

Figure 10
Arrange blocks in
rows as shown.

Step 3. Mark the top for quilting, if necessary. The quilt shown was quilted diagonally from corner to corner in the center squares of each block and in the ditch of all seams. The border was quilted in a geometric design.

Step 4. Sandwich batting between completed top and prepared backing piece. Safety-pin or baste layers together to hold flat.

Step 5. Quilt on marked lines and as desired. When quilting is complete, trim edges even and remove basting or pins.

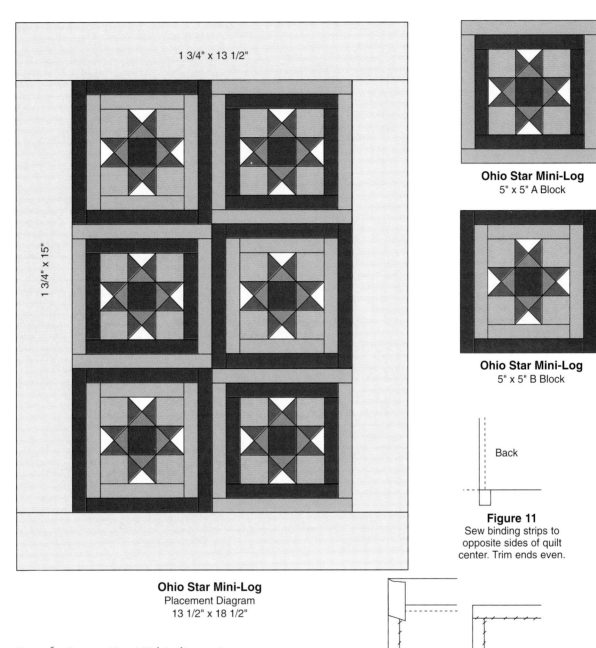

1 3/4" x 13 1/2"

1 3/4" x 15"

Ohio Star Mini-Log
Placement Diagram
13 1/2" x 18 1/2"

Ohio Star Mini-Log
5" x 5" A Block

Ohio Star Mini-Log
5" x 5" B Block

Back

Figure 11
Sew binding strips to
opposite sides of quilt
center. Trim ends even.

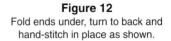

Figure 12
Fold ends under, turn to back and
hand-stitch in place as shown.

Step 6. Sew a 1" x 19" binding strip to opposite sides of the quilt center, extending the strip an equal amount on both ends, referring to Figure 11. Trim excess even with quilt top if needed. Fold over raw edge 1/4" and turn to backside. Hand-stitch in place.

Step 7. Sew the 1" x 16" strips to the remaining two sides as in Step 6. Trim ends to extend 3/8"

beyond end of quilt edge. Fold ends under as shown in Figure 12. Turn to back and hand-stitch in place to finish.

By Nancy Kiman

Log Cabins
for Christmas

Log Cabin quilts and projects using traditional red, green and white fabrics for the holiday season are fun to make.

In this section we have several stockings, a wall hanging, a full-size quilt and a few ornaments and gift bags. Each project was made using Log Cabin blocks.

If you like to decorate your home with quilted patchwork items, most of these projects are quick and easy so they could be made up in a short time.

Log Cabin Tree Skirt

What could be more appropriate as a tree skirt than a fabric tree?
The only problem is that you will cover it with gifts and no one will see how beautiful
it is! If you want people to notice it, finish it as a round table cover. Place it where
everyone will admire it during the Christmas season.

There are so many beautiful Christmas prints available to quilters these days. Metallics outline shapes, and the typical reds and greens have become burgundy and forest green for those who like subdued instead of bright shades.

Coordinated decorations are fun to create for yourself or as gifts for family and friends. Quilters are expected to have pretty stitched items all over the house during the holiday season. Wall hangings, quilts, ornaments, decorations for tables and more adorn the walls, tables, beds, the tree and even our doors.

Make these simple projects using Log Cabin blocks as the focus of the designs, and have fun creating gifts and decorations from the heart.

Cutting Instructions

Step 1. Cut two 2" by fabric width strips from each green. Cut strips to yield eight 3 1/2" and eight 5" segments from each color.

Step 2. Cut eight 4" x 4" squares white. Cut in half diagonally once.

Step 3. Cut 10 strips red print 2" by fabric width. Cut strips into 16 squares 2" x 2", 16 pieces 2" x 3 1/2", 16 pieces 2" x 8" and eight pieces each 2" x 11" and 2" x 9 1/2".

Quilt Specifications

Skill Level: Challenging
Quilt Size: Approximately 48" diameter
Block Size: 10 1/2" x 10 1/2"
Number of Blocks: 8

Materials

- 1 1/2 yards red print for sky
- 1 1/2 yards white-on-white print for snow
- 1/4 yard each 3 different greens for trees
- Scrap yellow or bonded lamé for stars
- 1" by fabric width strip brown for tree trunks
- 1 spool white all-purpose thread
- 1 spool gold metallic thread
- Batting 60" x 60"
- Backing 60" x 60"
- 6 yards self-made or purchased binding

Step 4. Cut eight yellow (or lamé) 2" x 2" squares.

Step 5. Cut four squares 8 1/2" x 8 1/2" from red print. Cut each square on the diagonal to make triangles. Cut one rectangle 21 1/2" x 15 1/2" and two 3 1/2" x 15 1/2" from red print.

Step 6. Cut four 16" x 16" squares and four 8 1/2" x 8 1/2" squares from white-on-white print. Cut each square in half on the diagonal to make triangles.

Piecing Blocks

Step 1. Turn the edges of the 1" by fabric width brown strip under 1/4" on each long side and press. ***Note:*** *Using a 1/2" bias strip bar makes this step easier.* Cut into 3" segments for tree trunks.

Step 2. Pin a tree-trunk strip onto eight of the small white-on-white triangles as shown in Figure 1. Stitch in place by hand or topstitch on each edge by machine. Trim point of strip to match triangle point.

Step 3. Sew a white triangle to each of the tree-trunk triangles to make a square as shown in Figure 2.

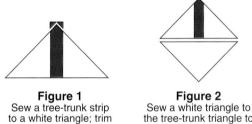

Figure 1
Sew a tree-trunk strip to a white triangle; trim top even as shown.

Figure 2
Sew a white triangle to the tree-trunk triangle to make a square.

Step 4. Sew the green and red print cut units together to make strips referring to Figure 3 for color arrangement. Sew a 2" yellow square to a 2" x 8" red print strip.

Step 5. Referring to Figure 4, sew the cut and pieced strips to the white-on-white tree base

Figure 3
Sew cut red print and green squares and rectangles together as shown. Sew yellow square to an 8" red print rectangle.

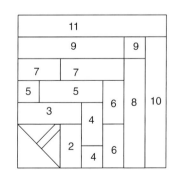

Figure 4
Piece Log Cabin Tree blocks in numerical order shown.

square in numerical order to piece Log Cabin Tree blocks. Complete eight blocks; press.

Step 6. To make B blocks, sew two red print triangles cut from 8 1/2" squares to the top of four tree blocks. Repeat with two white-on-white triangles cut from 8 1/2" squares on the bottom corners of the blocks referring to Figure 5.

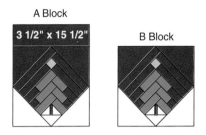

Figure 5
Sew red print and white-on-white triangles on corners of 4 tree blocks to make A and B blocks. Add 3 1/2" x 15 1/2" rectangle to tops of 2 blocks to make A blocks.

Step 7. To make A blocks, sew a 3 1/2" x 15 1/2" piece of red print to the tops of two of the blocks made in Step 6 referring to Figure 5. Set blocks aside.

Step 8. To make C blocks, sew a white-on-white triangle (cut from 16" x 16" squares) to the two bottom edges of the four remaining tree blocks, overlapping one corner, as shown in Figure 6.

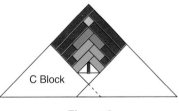

Figure 6
Sew large white-on-white triangles to corners of 4 tree blocks to make C blocks.

Assembly

Step 1. Arrange the A, B and C blocks with the red print 15 1/2" x 21 1/2" rectangle as shown in Figure 7. Sew the blocks in rows; join rows to complete center; press. ***Note:***

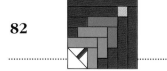

Don't worry if all edges do not line up as you will trim the project to an octagonal shape later.

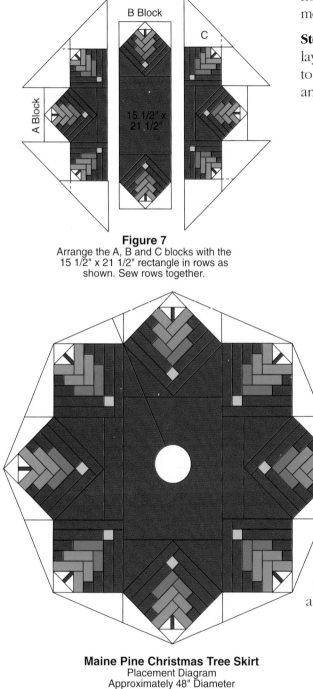

Figure 7
Arrange the A, B and C blocks with the
15 1/2" x 21 1/2" rectangle in rows as
shown. Sew rows together.

Maine Pine Christmas Tree Skirt
Placement Diagram
Approximately 48" Diameter

Step 2. Layer the backing fabric, batting and pieced top and pin-baste layers together to hold flat. Machine-quilt as desired with gold metallic thread.

Step 3. Trim edges in an octagon shape by laying a ruler from the point of one tree block to another. Draw a line 1/4" from that point and trim off excess referring to Figure 8.

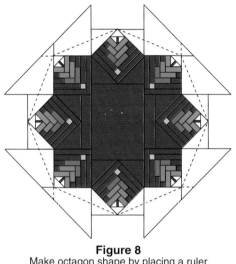

Figure 8
Make octagon shape by placing a ruler
from 1 tree base point to another and
adding 1/4" seam allowance.

Step 4. Slit one side to center between two trees. Cut a 5" circle in the center using any round object close in size (try a saucer from your kitchen cabinet).

Step 5. Bind edges with self-made or purchased binding all around center circle and edges to finish.

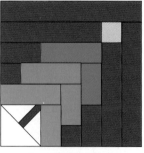

Log Cabin Tree
10 1/2" x 10 1/2" Block

Gift Bags & Ornaments

Decorating for Christmas is fun for quilters. Get out your red and green quilts and quilted wall hangings along with the quilted tree skirt, ornaments and gift bags. Recycling is fun with fabric gift bags. Ornaments make great little gifts for friends.

Log Cabin blocks can be combined to create several versions using the same stocking pattern. Gift bags are easy to make using one or more blocks, depending on the size of the gift. Be creative and make up many different bags to add color and a different texture to the collection of gifts under your tree.

If you like to embellish your projects, lace, rick-rack, buttons, ribbon and more may be added to your gift bags. Glitter paint can be used to personalize the bag for its recipient.

Instructions are given for two gifts bags and two ornaments. Create your own unique versions of these projects to add to the holiday festivities at your home this Christmas.

Gift Bag 1

Instructions

Step 1. Cut all white, red and green scraps into 1 1/2" strips. Sew a white strip to the right side of the preprint square. Trim strip even with square; press. Sew another white strip to the bottom of the preprint square; trim strip even with square and press.

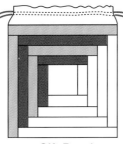

Gift Bag 1
Placement Diagram
11" x 13"

Gift Bag Specifications	
Skill Level: Easy	**Bag Size:** 11" x 13"
Block Size: 11" x 11"	**Number of Blocks:** 1

Materials

- 13" x 15" backing fabric
- 1 preprint square 3 1/2" x 3 1/2"
- Scraps white, green and red Christmas prints
- All-purpose thread to match fabrics
- 1 yard red 1/4" satin ribbon
- 2 small bells

Step 2. Add a red strip to the left side and top of the preprint square. Continue adding strips, alternating the red and green strips on the dark side of the block as shown in Figure 1. Press and square up finished block to 11" x 11".

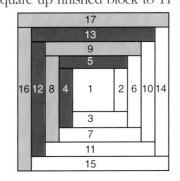

Figure 1
Piece 1 block using 1 1/2" stripes for gift bag as shown.

Step 3. Cut a piece of white print 4 1/2" x 11 1/2". Sew the strip to the top of the block.

Step 4. Place the finished block on the backing fabric with right sides together. Trim backing even with pieced front. Stitch around three sides, leaving top edge open.

Step 5. Turn bag right side out. Press under 1/4" on top edge of bag and stitch in place. Turn top edge under 2" and stitch along bottom edge. Sew two lines of stitching 1/2" apart and 3/4" from top edge of bag to make a channel to place ribbon for drawstring.

Step 6. Unstitch side seam between stitching lines. Cut ribbon into two equal lengths. Put a small pin on one end of one ribbon and draw through the channel on the front. Repeat with the second piece of ribbon in the back channel.

Step 7. Tie a bell to each end of one ribbon. Tie the two ends of the ribbon on each end together to make loops of the ribbon on each end. Pull ribbons to gather the top of the bag closed after placing gift inside.

Gift Bag 2

Gift Bag Specifications

Skill Level: Easy **Bag Size:** 10 1/2" x 13 1/2"
Block Size: 7 1/2" x 10 1/2"
Number of Blocks: 1

Materials

- 13" x 15" backing fabric
- Scraps white, green and red Christmas prints
- All-purpose thread to match fabrics
- 1 yard gold metallic cording

Instructions

Step 1. Cut all white, red and green scraps into 1 1/4" strips. Cut two white print pieces 2" long. Sew the two pieces together for center. Cut two red print pieces 2" long. Sew to top and bottom of white strips referring to Figure 2. Cut two

green print pieces 2" long. Sew to the top and bottom.

Step 2. Continue adding white strips to sides and alternating the addition of red and green print strips to the top and bottom to complete one block as shown in Figures 3 and 4.

Step 3. Press and square up finished block to 8" x 11". Cut two green print strips 2" x 11". Sew a strip to the white sides of the block. Cut one green print strip 2" x 10 1/2". Sew to the bottom of the block; press.

Figure 2
Sew a red piece and a green piece to the top and bottom of the white pieces.

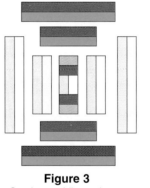

Figure 3
Continue adding strips to the center to complete the block as shown.

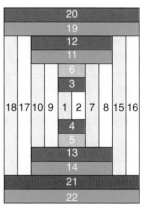

Figure 4
Piece 1 block using 1 1/4" strips for gift bag as shown.

Step 4. Cut a piece of green print 4 1/2" x 10 1/2". Sew the strip to the top of the block.

Step 5. Finish as for Gift Bag 1, Steps 4–7, except use gold cording instead of ribbon and eliminate the bells.

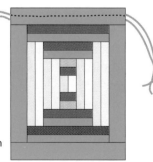

Gift Bag 2
Placement Diagram
10 1/2" x 13 1/2"

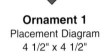

Ornament 1

Ornament Specifications

Skill Level: Easy
Ornament Size: 4 1/2" x 4 1/2"
Number of Blocks: 2

Materials

- Scraps white, green and red Christmas prints
- All-purpose thread to match fabrics
- 12" red 1/4" satin ribbon
- Small amount of polyester fiberfill

Instructions

Step 1. Use full-size block drawing given in Figure 13 to create templates or as a paper-piecing foundation for piecing the small Log Cabin blocks. Remember to reverse the drawing as lines will be on the back-side of the finished block. See Page 150 for paper-piecing instructions.

Step 2. If using strip-piecing method, cut scraps into 1 1/4"-wide strips. Start in the center with a red and a white 1 1/4" square. Add strips in numerical order referring to Figure 13.

Step 3. Complete two blocks. Place right sides together and sew around outside edges leaving a 2 1/2" opening on one side. Turn right side out through the opening.

Step 4. Stuff bits of polyester stuffing inside

through the opening. When stuffing is complete, hand-stitch opening closed.

Step 5. Tie a bow and a loop in the ribbon and hand-stitch to one corner for hanging.

Ornament 1
Placement Diagram
4 1/2" x 4 1/2"

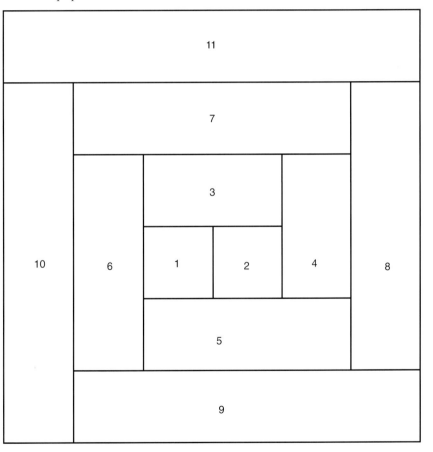

Figure 5
Full-size drawing of Ornament 1 block.

Ornament 2

Step 5. Turn edges of backing under 1/4" and bring to front to finish edges. Topstitch in place by hand or machine to hold.

Step 6. Glue the hanger to the back of the ornament to hold in place.

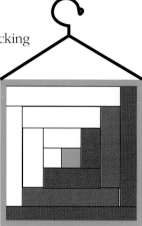

Ornament 2
Placement Diagram
3 1/2" x 3 1/2"

Instructions

Step 1. Use full-size block drawing given in Figure 6 to create templates or as a paper-piecing foundation for piecing the small Log Cabin block. Remember to reverse the drawing as lines will be on the backside of the finished block. See Page 150 for paper-piecing instructions.

Step 2. If using strip-piecing method, cut scraps into 1"-wide strips. Start in the center with a green and a white 1" square. Add strips in numerical order referring to Figure 6.

Step 3. Complete one block. Press and square up to 3 1/2" x 3 1/2".

Step 4. Place backing piece right side down; center batting piece on top. Center the pieced block on top of these layers. The backing will extend evenly all around.

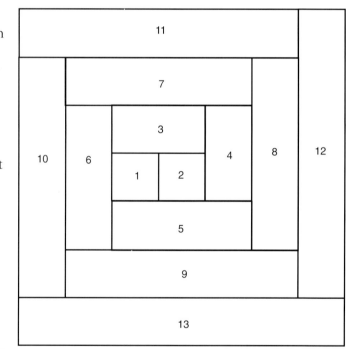

Figure 6
Full-size drawing of Ornament 2 block.

Christmas Stockings

Decorating for Christmas is fun for quilters.
Who can resist making one of these large stockings?

Log Cabin blocks can be combined to create several versions using the same stocking pattern.

Instructions are given for the three basic stockings. Create your own unique versions of these projects to add to the holiday festivities at your home this Christmas.

The stocking pattern is too large to fit on a back page. Rather than provide a graph to enlarge, a full-size pattern is given in sections. Draw sections onto a large piece of paper to create the full-size pattern.

Stocking 1

Instructions

Step 1. Trace each shape given with the stocking pattern on Pages xxxx onto plain paper; transfer all numbers. Cut out paper pieces; match numbers and tape paper pieces together, adding 10" in length between the 1 and 3 numbered pieces. Refer to Figure 1a pn Page 100 for layout of pieces.

Step 2. Cut two stocking shapes from velvet and two from lining fabric, adding a 1/4" seam allowance all around when cutting. ***Note:*** *Layer the lining fabric with right sides together when cutting to get a top and back piece. The velvet*

Stocking Specifications
Skill Level: Easy   **Stocking Size:** 14" x 20"
Block Size: 5" x 5"
Number of Blocks: 1

Materials
• 2/3 yard red velvet
• 1/2 yard lining fabric
• Scraps off-white and green prints
• All-purpose thread to match fabrics
• 1 spool gold metallic thread
• 15" metallic braid
• 1 sewing machine ornament
• Fabric glue

pieces should be cut one at a time; reverse pattern when cutting one shape. Remember that velvet has a nap. Cut both stockings with the nap running in the same direction.

Step 3. Set aside the stocking back and the lining pieces.

Step 4. Cut one strip each green and off-white prints 1" by fabric width. Cut one square 1 1/2" x 1 1/2" off-white print for center. Sew the square to the green strip; trim strip even with square. Sew this unit to the green strip again; trim strip even with square. Continue adding

Stocking 1
Placement Diagram
14"x 20"

Stocking 2
Placement Diagram
14"x 20"

Stocking 3
Placement Diagram
14"x 20"

By Nancy Kiman

strips around the center referring to Figure 1 for order of piecing. Add four logs of each color on each side.

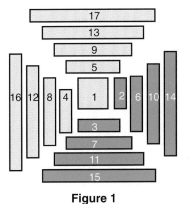

Figure 1
Add strips to center in the order and colors shown.

Step 5. Press block and square up to 5" x 5". Pin diagonally on the velvet stocking front referring to the Placement Diagram.

Step 6. Using metallic thread in the top of the machine and all-purpose thread in the bobbin, machine satin-stitch around outside edges of the block to secure to stocking.

Step 7. With right sides together, sew the velvet stocking pieces together; repeat for lining pieces. Turn each right side out. Press the lining piece. **Note:** *It is difficult to press velvet without a needleboard, a special pressing tool for velvet. Place a heavy towel on the ironing surface and press from the wrong side with velvet touching the towel, if necessary.*

Step 8. Place lining inside velvet stocking with wrong sides together. Measure around the top edges of the stocking. Cut a piece of off-white

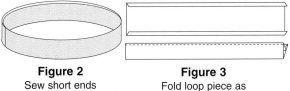

Figure 2
Sew short ends together and fold with wrong sides together to make cuff piece.

Figure 3
Fold loop piece as shown.

print that measurement plus 1/2" and 7" wide for top cuff.

Step 9. Sew short ends of cuff together to form a tube; press seam open. Fold this in half with wrong sides together as shown in Figure 2.

Step 10. Cut an 8" piece of off-white fabric 1 1/2" wide. Press 1/4" in on each long edge. Fold again to make a long finished strip. Stitch close to edge to finish for hanging loop as shown in Figure 3.

Step 11. Fold the strip in half to form a loop and pin to lining top at heel side seam with raw edges together.

Step 12. Aligning all raw edges, pin the cuff piece to the top edge of stocking on the inside lining edge, pinning through both velvet and lining. **Note:** *The folded loop piece will be between the lining and the cuff piece.*

Step 13. Sew cuff to stocking; press cuff up and down over the outside velvet edge to complete the cuff. Topstitch over loop area to secure.

Step 14. Tie a bow with the metallic braid. Glue it and the ornament to the top of the Log Cabin block to finish.

Stocking 2

Stocking Specifications
Skill Level: Easy   **Stocking Size:** 14" x 20"
Block Size: 5 1/4" x 5 1/4"
Number of Blocks: 10

Materials
• 1/8 yard each 3 light and 3 dark Christmas prints
• 1/2 yard lining fabric
• 1 strip red print or solid 1 1/4" x 15"
• 1 piece red print 7" x 20"
• All-purpose thread to match fabrics

Instructions

Step 1. Cut 1 1/4" by fabric width strips from both light and dark Christmas prints.

Step 2. Sew a light print strip to the red 1 1/4" x 15" strip. Cut off excess light print. Press seam to dark fabric; cut in 1 1/4" segments. You will need 10 segments.

Step 3. Sew the segments from Step 2 to a light print strip. Trim strip even with segments as shown in Figure 4. Continue adding strips in numerical order and in colors shown in Figure 5. Complete 10 blocks.

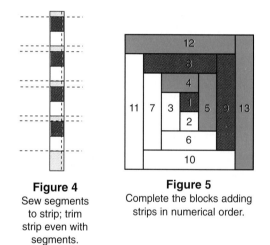

Figure 4
Sew segments to strip; trim strip even with segments.

Figure 5
Complete the blocks adding strips in numerical order.

Step 4. Arrange the blocks in two rows of four blocks each. Join in rows; join the rows. Sew the remaining two blocks together and add to bottom of pieced rows referring to Figure 6.

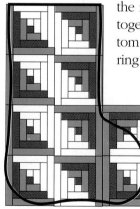

Figure 6
Arrange the pieced blocks and sew together as shown for stocking front.

Step 5. Use full-size stocking pattern (see Pages 91–93) to cut stocking shape from the stitched Log Cabin blocks. ***Note:*** *Blocks are larger than stocking when stitched together and some complete strips may be trimmed off when cutting stocking shape.*

Step 6. Cut one backing piece, reversing the pattern. Cut two lining pieces, reversing one.

Step 7. Sew stocking together; add cuff and loop to finish as in Steps 7–13 of Stocking 1.

Stocking 3

Stocking Specifications
Skill Level: Easy   **Stocking Size:** 14" x 20"
Block Size: 5" x 5"
Number of Blocks: 4

Materials
• 1/2 yard green print • 1/2 yard lining fabric • Scraps off-white and red prints • All-purpose thread to match fabrics • 12" red satin 1/4" ribbon

Instructions

Step 1. Cut two strips red print 1" by fabric width. Cut two strips off-white print 1 1/2" by fabric width.

Step 2. Cut two pieces from one red strip 5" long. Sew the two pieces together; press seam open. Cut into four 1" segments for center. Sew these segments to a red strip; trim strip even with segments.

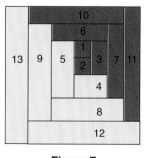

Figure 7
Complete 4 blocks adding wider off-white strips to 1 side of center and narrow red print strips to the other side. Sew in numerical order.

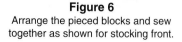

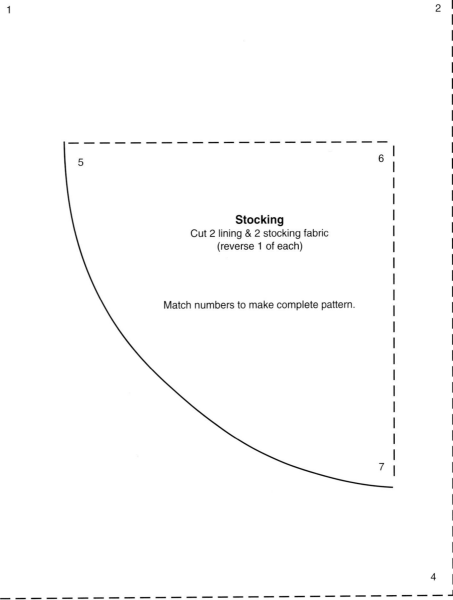

Figure 8
Place 2 blocks at the top edge of the stocking, 1 on the toe and 1 one on the heel.

Step 3. Sew these pieced units to an off-white strip; trim strip even with segments. Continue adding strips to the segments to create four off-center Log Cabin blocks as shown in Figure 7.

Step 4. Cut two lining and two green print stockings, reversing one of each.

Step 5. Sew two Log Cabin blocks together referring to Figure 8 for color placement. Fold under 1/4" on bottom edge and press. Place the blocks on the top of the stocking front piece. Stitch across bottom folded edge to attach to stocking. Baste across top edge.

Step 6. Press 1/4" under on the off-white edges of the two remaining blocks. Place one block on the heel and one on the toe section of

stocking front, extending red side of block off edges of stocking, as in Figure 8.

Step 7. Machine-stitch heel and toe blocks to stocking along folded edge of blocks to secure. Baste around outside edges of stocking. Trim blocks even with curved area of stocking.

Step 8. Place lining pieces with right sides together; stitch around sides, leaving top edges

1

2

5

6

Stocking
Cut 2 lining & 2 stocking fabric
(reverse 1 of each)

Match numbers to make complete pattern.

7

5

4

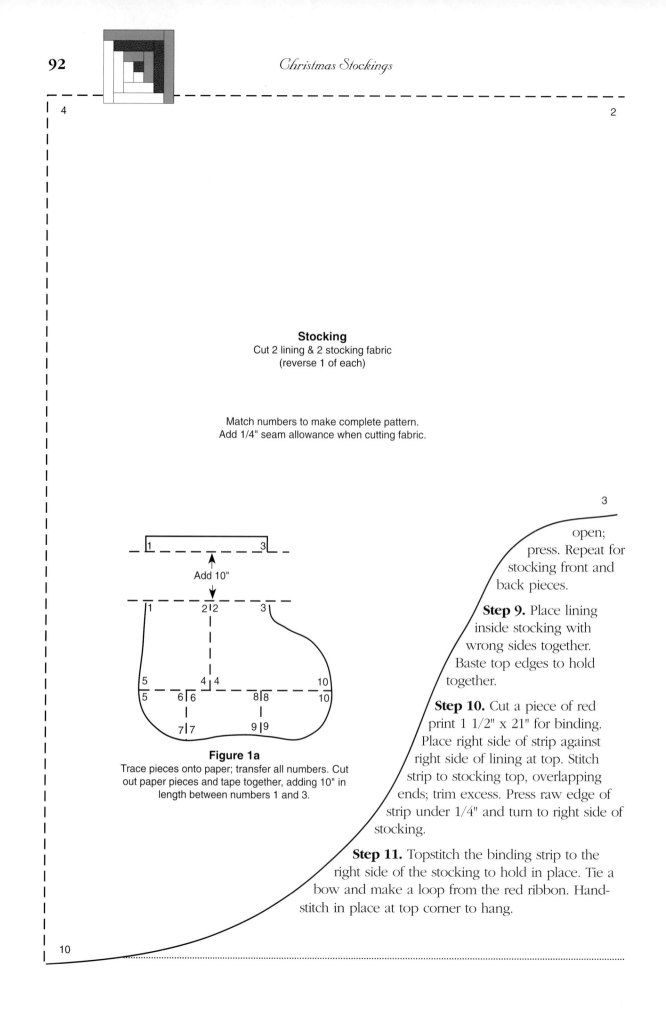

4

2

Stocking
Cut 2 lining & 2 stocking fabric
(reverse 1 of each)

Match numbers to make complete pattern.
Add 1/4" seam allowance when cutting fabric.

3

1   3

Add 10"

1   2 2   3

5   4 4   10
5   6 6   8 8   10

7 7   9 9

Figure 1a
Trace pieces onto paper; transfer all numbers. Cut
out paper pieces and tape together, adding 10" in
length between numbers 1 and 3.

open;
press. Repeat for
stocking front and
back pieces.

Step 9. Place lining
inside stocking with
wrong sides together.
Baste top edges to hold
together.

Step 10. Cut a piece of red
print 1 1/2" x 21" for binding.
Place right side of strip against
right side of lining at top. Stitch
strip to stocking top, overlapping
ends; trim excess. Press raw edge of
strip under 1/4" and turn to right side of
stocking.

Step 11. Topstitch the binding strip to the
right side of the stocking to hold in place. Tie a
bow and make a loop from the red ribbon. Hand-
stitch in place at top corner to hang.

10

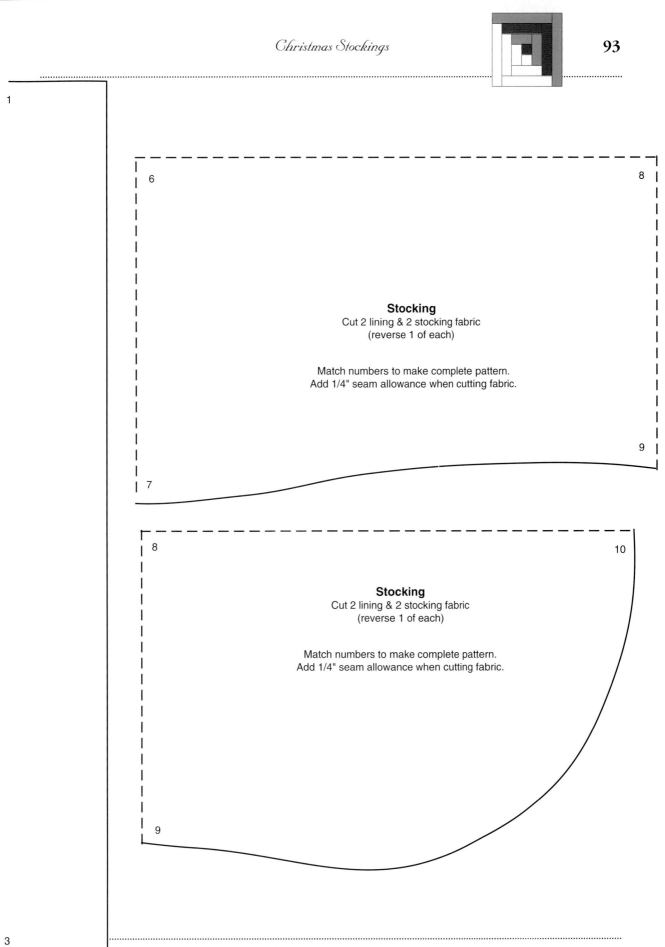

1

6   8

Stocking
Cut 2 lining & 2 stocking fabric
(reverse 1 of each)

Match numbers to make complete pattern.
Add 1/4" seam allowance when cutting fabric.

9

7

8   10

Stocking
Cut 2 lining & 2 stocking fabric
(reverse 1 of each)

Match numbers to make complete pattern.
Add 1/4" seam allowance when cutting fabric.

9

3

By Joyce Mori

Log Cabin for Christmas

A number of years ago I took a Log Cabin workshop from a quilt teacher named Barb Ludewig. She is an exuberant, energetic instructor and our class was a lot of fun. The main point of the class was to teach us how to make the center Nine-Patch block on this quilt in a quick and easy way.

Several years went by and I was cleaning up my quilt room when I discovered this half-started quilt. I could not remember a thing about the construction of the quilt, but I liked the few blocks that were complete and I decided to finish this as my Christmas quilt. I had recently purchased the Easy Angle by Sharon Hultgren, and I use it all the time to make triangles. So I used it to quickly make the small triangles for this quilt, and I actually completed the top. Now I have to quilt it!

The block is actually a Chimneys and Cornerstones block. It is divided into half light and half dark, both in the strips and center Nine-Patch. If you look at Figure 1, you will see that the light half of the Nine-Patch has dark strips on its side and the dark half of the Nine-Patch has light strips on its side. All the blocks should have been pieced with the same fabric; however, because I did this project in two stages, several years apart, I did not have enough fabric to make all of them identical, but this is not really noticeable.

The setting is original as far as I know. Most *Log Cabin* quilts have an equal number of blocks on each side, but I wanted a rectangular quilt that would better fit a bed. I laid the blocks out on the floor and kept moving them around for several days until I found something

Quilt Specifications

Skill Level: Intermediate
Quilt Size: 72" x 90"   **Block Size:** 9" x 9"
Number of Blocks: 80

Materials

- 1/3 yard dark green #1
- 1 fat quarter (18" x 22") each dark green #2, light green #2, dark red #3
- 2 yards dark green #3
- 1 yard medium green
- 1/3 yard light green #1
- 1 1/3 yards dark red #1
- 2 1/4 yards dark red #2
- 1 1/8 yards light gray #1
- 2 yards light gray #2
- 2 yards light gray #3
- Backing 76" x 94"
- Batting 76" x 94"
- All-purpose thread to match fabrics

I liked. I do think that the center squares, with the concentration of the dark red and green fabrics, help reinforce the Christmas feeling of the quilt.

Instructions

Step 1. Prepare a template using pattern piece

given. Cut as directed on the pattern. Sew a light green #1 triangle to a dark green #1 triangle to make a square. Repeat to complete 160 squares.

Step 2. Cut all remaining fabrics into 1 1/2" by fabric width strips.

Step 3. To complete center Nine-Patch units, cut six medium green strips into 1 1/2" squares. You will need 160 squares.

Step 4. Sew three medium green and dark green #2 strips together; cut into 1 1/2" segments as shown in Figure 1; you will need 80 segments. Sew a segment to one pieced triangle/square unit as shown in Figure 2.

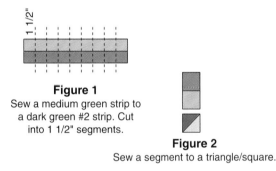

Figure 1
Sew a medium green strip to
a dark green #2 strip. Cut
into 1 1/2" segments.

Figure 2
Sew a segment to a triangle/square.

Step 5. Repeat with the same number of light green #2 and medium green strips; cut into 1 1/2" segments as shown in Figure 3. Sew a segment to one pieced triangle/square unit as shown in Figure 4. Repeat for 80 units.

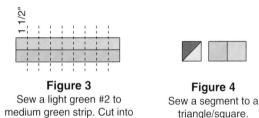

Figure 3
Sew a light green #2 to
medium green strip. Cut into
1 1/2" segments.

Figure 4
Sew a segment to a
triangle/square.

Step 5. Sew a medium green strip to a dark red #3 strip to a medium green strip three times. Cut strips into 1 1/2" segments referring to Figure 5. You will need 80 segments.

Step 6. Arrange the pieced units in rows referring to Figure 6. Join in rows; join the rows to complete the center Nine-Patch units; press.

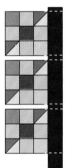

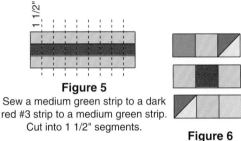

Figure 5
Sew a medium green strip to a dark
red #3 strip to a medium green strip.
Cut into 1 1/2" segments.

Figure 6
Arrange the pieced units in rows;
join to make Nine-Patch centers.

Step 7. Sew the Nine-Patch units to a dark red #1 strip as shown in Figure 7. Chain-piece to strip until all Nine-Patch centers have been used. Trim strip even with Nine-Patch center as shown in Figure 8; press.

Figure 7
Sew the Nine-Patch units
to a dark red #1 strip.

Figure 8
Trim strip even with
Nine-Patch units.

Step 8. Sew the Nine-Patch centers to another dark red #1 strip; trim and press as before.

Step 9. Continue adding strips around center referring to Figure 9 for color placement and sewing order. Complete 80 blocks.

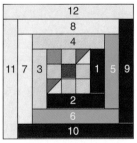

Figure 9
Add strips to blocks in the
color order shown
referring to the Color Key.
Complete 80 blocks.

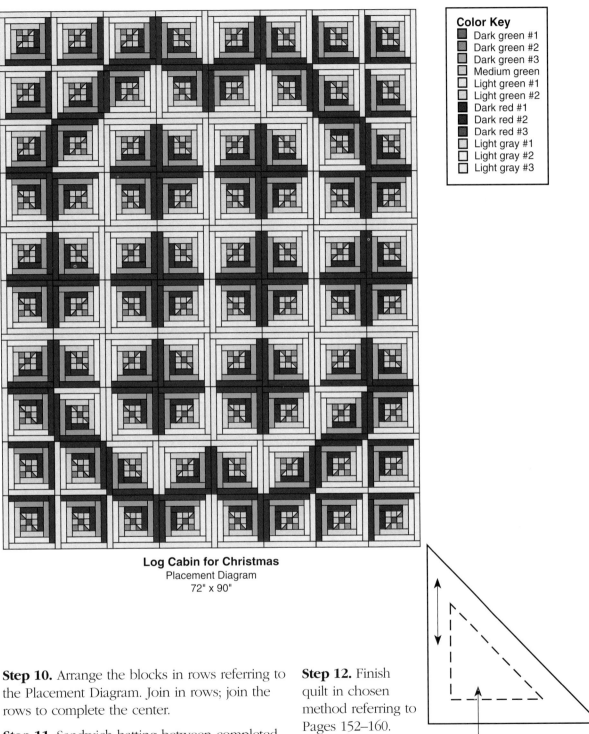

Log Cabin for Christmas
Placement Diagram
72" x 90"

Color Key
- Dark green #1
- Dark green #2
- Dark green #3
- Medium green
- Light green #1
- Light green #2
- Dark red #1
- Dark red #2
- Dark red #3
- Light gray #1
- Light gray #2
- Light gray #3

Step 10. Arrange the blocks in rows referring to the Placement Diagram. Join in rows; join the rows to complete the center.

Step 11. Sandwich batting between completed top and prepared backing piece. Safety-pin or baste layers together to hold flat.

Step 12. Finish quilt in chosen method referring to Pages 152–160.

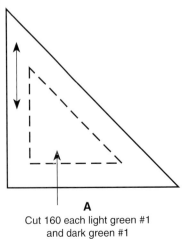

A
Cut 160 each light green #1
and dark green #1

By Sandra L. Hatch

Santa's Log Cabin

Buying Christmas gifts for each member of a large and still-growing family can be expensive. Instead of giving up the tradition, one of my sisters had a great idea how we could continue to give something special without spending too much money: make something.

Because I am the quilter in my family, it is more or less expected that whoever's name I draw will receive some kind of quilted project. So far I haven't failed them.

One year I made a quilted jacket; another year I made a full-size *Log Cabin* quilt. In recent years my gift has been a table cover or a wall hanging. The wall hanging shown here was my latest gift, and the chosen sister was thrilled to get it.

We have already drawn our names for next year and, as usual, I will be working on my gift the night before giving it away. It's no fun otherwise.

Instructions

Step 1. Cut one strip 1 1/2" by fabric width each from red and green prints. Sew a red strip to a green strip as shown in Figure 1; press

Quilt Specifications

Skill Level: Intermediate   **Quilt Size:** 29" x 36"
Block Size: 7" x 7" Log Cabin; 5" x 12" Santa
Number of Blocks: 1 Santa; 10 Log Cabin

Materials

- 1 fat quarter-yard each of 4 red and 4 green prints
- 1/4 yard dark green print (Santa and borders)
- 1/4 yard red solid
- Scrap of peach-tone fabric 3" x 6"
- Scrap of white 4" x 5"
- Scraps of red print for Santa
- 1 red and 2 black 1/4" buttons
- Backing 33" x 40"
- Batting 33" x 40"
- 4 yards self-made or purchased binding

seam to dark side. Cut apart at 1 1/2" intervals as shown in Figure 2.

Step 2. Cut one strip of another green print 1 1/2" by the fabric width; sew the previously

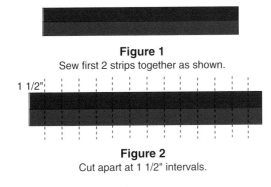

Figure 1
Sew first 2 strips together as shown.

Figure 2
Cut apart at 1 1/2" intervals.

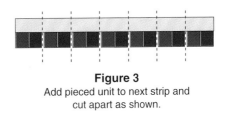

Figure 3
Add pieced unit to next strip and cut apart as shown.

sewn units to this strip and cut apart as shown in Figure 3.

Step 3. Continue cutting strips and sewing in this fashion until you have 10 blocks as shown in the Log Cabin piecing diagram. Set the blocks aside.

Step 4. To piece the center Santa design, prepare templates using pattern pieces given. Cut as directed on each piece. Sew B and BR to A; sew C to E. Sew D to F and DR to FR; join the two units and add G. Set the C-E unit into the D-F-G unit and add the A-B unit to the top to complete the block as shown in Figure 4.

Step 5. Cut two strips 1 1/2" x 5 1/2" and two strips 1 1/2" x 12 1/2" from red solid. Cut four H squares from dark green print; sew one to each end of the shorter red strips. Add the long strips to the sides of the pieced Santa; add the strips with H to the top and bottom to complete the Santa section as shown in Figure 5.

Step 6. Lay out the completed Log Cabin blocks and the Santa block referring to the Placement Diagram.

Step 7. Sew together to complete the inner portion of the top; press. Sew button nose and eyes on Santa.

Step 8. Cut two border strips 1 1/2" x 21 1/2" from dark green print; add to top and bottom. Cut two more strips 1 1/2" x 30 1/2"; add to sides. Press seams toward border strips.

Step 9. Cut two strips red solid 1" x 23 1/2" for top and bottom and two strips 1" x 31 1/2" for sides. Sew shorter strips to top and bottom and longer strips to sides; press seams toward border.

Step 10. Cut two strips dark green 3" x 24 1/2" for top and bottom and 3" x 36 1/2" for sides. Sew to pieced center; press seams toward border.

Step 11. Sandwich batting between completed top and prepared backing piece. Safety-pin or baste layers together to hold flat.

Step 12. Finish quilt in chosen method referring to Pages 152–160.

Figure 4
Piece units and join to complete Santa block as shown.

Figure 5
Sew strips and squares to Santa unit as shown. Seam allowances are not included in measurements.

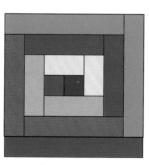

Log Cabin
7" x 7" Block

Santa
5" x 12" Block

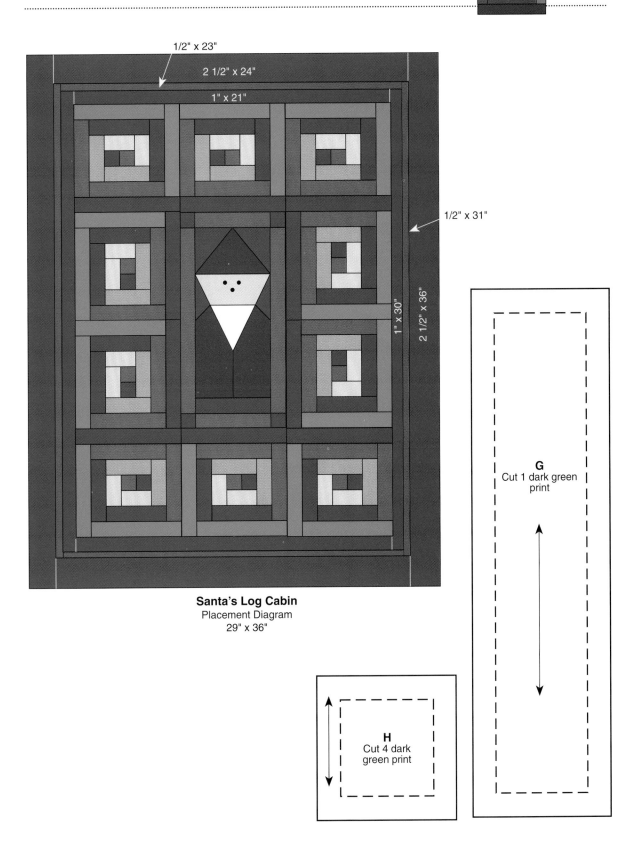

1/2" x 23"

2 1/2" x 24"

1" x 21"

1/2" x 31"

1" x 30"

2 1/2" x 36"

Santa's Log Cabin
Placement Diagram
29" x 36"

G
Cut 1 dark green print

H
Cut 4 dark green print

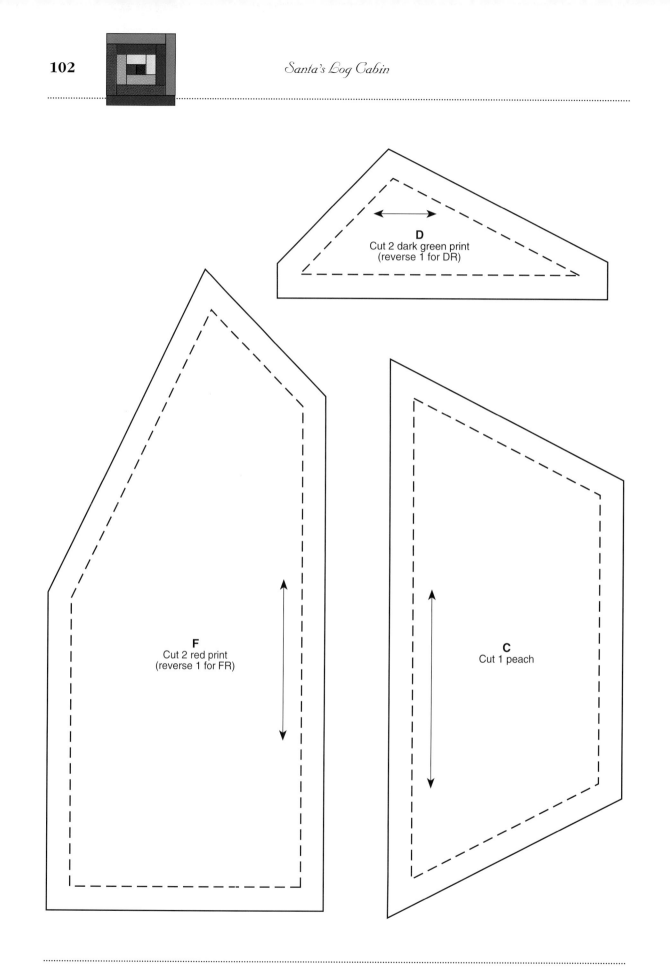

D
Cut 2 dark green print
(reverse 1 for DR)

F
Cut 2 red print
(reverse 1 for FR)

C
Cut 1 peach

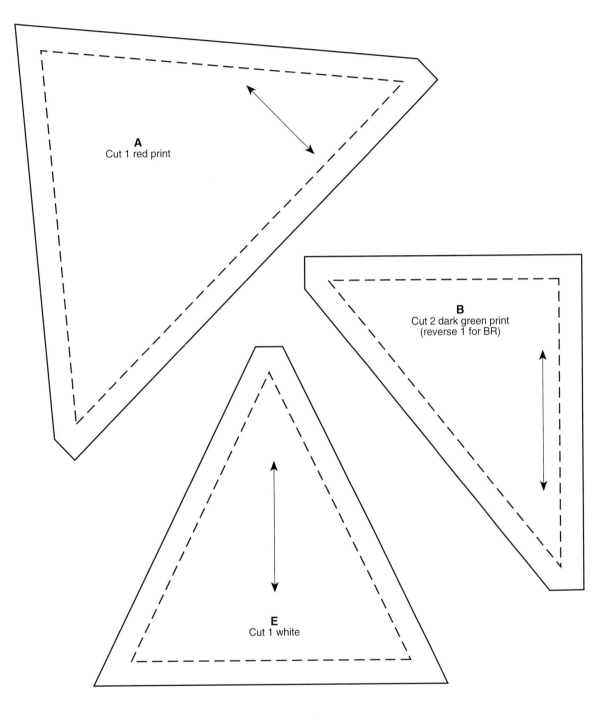

A
Cut 1 red print

B
Cut 2 dark green print
(reverse 1 for BR)

E
Cut 1 white

By Melody Johnson

Contemporary
Log Cabin Quilts

Like every other pattern Log Cabins have been adapted by quiltmakers down through the years. Many have taken this classic design and added their own original touch.

Whether it is a crazy quilt using the latest techniques, a child's Scottie dog quilt stitched with plaid, or a foundation-pieced quilt with a new twist, these projects have a look all their own.

Let yourself go and play with some of these new methods, techniques and designs!

Lollapalooza Log Cabin

My first attempt at quiltmaking was a queen-size pink-and-blue Log Cabin. It couldn't have been more traditional. I made one hundred 12-inch blocks and arranged and rearranged the settings until I finally settled on the Barn Raising design. I sewed the strips by machine and quilted it by hand in a hoop.

On that first Log Cabin quilt I used a percale sheet for the backing, and because the weave was so tight, my fingers really ached, pushing the needle without the aid of a thimble. I did just about everything the hard way with that quilt, including cutting the strips with a pair of shears because I was not aware of the wonders of rotary cutting.

The essential thriftiness of the Log Cabin is another reason I love it. In that first quilt I used an assembly-line method in which I sewed my strips end to end so that I had one endless strip to sew to my blocks. These days I am not nearly so concerned with thriftiness. I use up leftovers in crazy-patch Log Cabin blocks, which become wildly colorful baby quilts, wall quilts and garments. We still sleep under that first Log Cabin, and threadbare as it is, I still love it.

My interest in the Log Cabin was recently rekindled by the exhibit of Log Cabin quilts at the Museum of the American Quilter's Society in Paducah, Ky.

Several of my friends participated in that show and I wanted to join in on the fun. After a few weeks of pondering, I came up with a design that I could get excited about making. It had to be original, unpredictable and colorful. My design was based on really skewed blocks

Quilt Specifications

Skill Level: Easy

Quilt Size: Any size

Block Size: Any size

Number of Blocks: Any number

Materials

- EZ Tear fabric stabilizer* or lightweight paper large enough to produce the desired size quilt
- Fabric scraps from your collection
- Backing 4" larger than finished top all around
- Cotton batting 4" larger than finished top all around
- All-purpose thread to match fabrics
- Self-made or purchased binding

*EZ Tear from Graphic Impressions, 1741 Masters Ln., Lexington, KY 40515, (606) 273–1507.

which, despite their angularity, still managed to align exactly in the finished quilt.

I am not a quilter who enjoys matching seams; in fact, I have made a career out of ignoring designs which call for perfection. For this particular design to work I needed a construction method that was easy and fun for me and, in turn, for you.

I found a great product called EZ Tear from

Lollapalooza Log Cabin
Placement Diagram
Any Size

Graphic Impressions. It is 50" wide and I like to have a 50-yard roll on hand for use as a stabilizer for machine embroidery, although I think it is primarily used to trace templates for flip-and-sew quilt blocks.

I drew my quilt full size on EZ Tear and, beginning in the center of each block, I chose to place my most vibrant colors to build each block. Since I was using my own dye-painted fabrics, plus black, there was no point in planning the color scheme, as the color shifts dramatically within each piece. I used my standard color plan—all color, all the time.

As long as I sewed each strip exactly on the drawn line I was assured that the finished quilt would line up. The color choices I made during the construction were based on the colors in the neighboring block.

I made the first one and then looked for fabrics for the neighboring block which would contrast wildly with those first fabrics. I love placing color opposites next to each other: Yellow and

purple, turquoise and orange, green and red—all of these combinations give me a visual thrill. I use black as an organizing element, a way of controlling the color riot.

I so enjoyed designing this quilt that I made a second and a third, each a new variation on the theme. When I teach my students this method, I encourage them to make their own original quilt, using colors and block variations that reflect their own individuality. I believe we are all unique, and we have an opportunity to express that creative quality in our quiltmaking.

Instructions

Step 1. Decide on size of finished quilt. ***Note: The EZ Tear product is 50" wide. For larger quilts, work in sections to make desired size.*** Draw a rectangle on the EZ Tear product in your chosen size. Divide the space of the rectangle by drawing two non-parallel vertical lines. Then draw two non-parallel horizontal lines referring to Figure 1. The point at which the lines intersect is called the axis. The point at which a line meets the edge of the rectangle is called the end point.

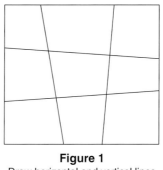

Figure 1
Draw horizontal and vertical lines
on a rectangle as shown.

Step 2. Draw boxes around axis points as shown in Figure 2.

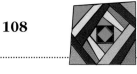

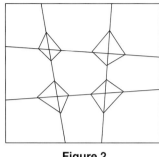

Figure 2
Draw boxes at axis points.

Step 3. Draw half-diamonds at end points as shown in Figure 3.

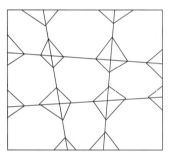

Figure 3
Draw half-diamonds at end points.

Step 4. Draw angled lines in four corners of the rectangle as shown in Figure 4.

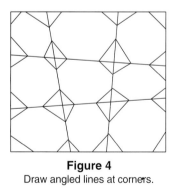

Figure 4
Draw angled lines at corners.

Step 5. Draw logs surrounding the boxed axis

points referring to Figure 5. ***Note:*** *It is OK if logs overlap.*

Step 6. Draw logs surrounding half-diamonds at end points and angled corner lines referring again to Figure 5.

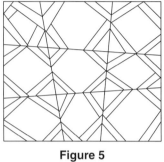

Figure 5
Draw logs around boxed axis points
and at end points and corners.

Step 7. Continue drawing logs to fill in the spaces as shown in Figure 6, or fill in the

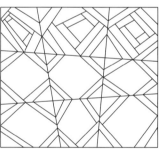

Figure 6
Continue drawing logs to fill spaces.

Figure 7
Use a favorite block to fill space.

spaces using one of your favorite blocks as shown in Figure 7.

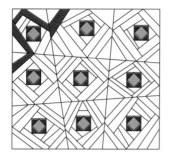

Figure 8
Create an internal border using black or dark fabric around shapes as shown.

Step 8. Number each block and mark the top. The color scheme can be the most important element of the design. Use color to emphasize the axis points or the centers of the blocks; or create an internal border as shown in Figure 8.

Step 9. Cut the drawing into blocks. Choose scraps from your scrap basket; choose a center piece from the scraps for piece 1. Place this piece with piece 2 on top on backside of stabilizer as for foundation-piecing on Page 150. Sew along line on foundation. ***Note:*** *Remember*

to leave a 1/4" seam allowance beyond the edge of the foundation for seam allowance to join blocks.

Step 10. Continue adding scraps to foundation in order around the center to complete the block; repeat for the required number of blocks.

Step 11. Arrange the blocks back in the original formation. Join the blocks in rows; join the rows to complete the quilt center.

Step 12. A border or multiple borders may be added to the completed center to contain it, or it may be bound and finished as is. The quilt shown was bound with self-made binding using scraps of many colors sewn together to create one long strip.

Step 13. Finish in chosen method referring to instructions on Pages 152–160.

Tips & Techniques

Cotton batting is preferred for this crazy-type method of making Log Cabin quilts. Cotton batting adheres to cotton fabrics. Iron the layers together before basting and quilting to prevent puckers and pleats in the finished quilt.

By Kaye Wood

Crystal Star Wall Quilt

Diamonds and stars have always intrigued quilters, probably because of the dimensional possibilities of the diamonds. Combining Log Cabin techniques with diamond shapes to make a star adds even more interest. Log Cabin diamonds look difficult, but just follow these steps to see how easy they can be.

Sewing strips around a center diamond in a sequence similar to making square Log Cabin blocks results in a Log Cabin star point. Like traditional blocks, varying the width of the strips creates a different look.

Using a special tool to ensure accuracy makes what seems like a difficult task easy. If you use the Starmaker 8™ tool as directed, you might like the results so much Log Cabin stars of all sizes will be forthcoming.

Follow the instructions given for sewing, pressing and cutting to create a unique Log Cabin design.

Instructions

Note: *Cut all strips the size given by the fabric's width. Use 1/4" seams for all stitching. To press accurately: Do not use steam; steam can stretch the strips; press across the width of the fabric strip to eliminate stretching; press from the right side of the fabric to eliminate pleats at the seam line.*

Step 1. Cut the following strips: three 1 1/2" strips blue solid for 1 and 2; four strips light teal solid 2 1/2" for 3 and 4; four strips purple moiré 1 1/2" for 5 and 6; five strips dark teal solid 2 1/2" for 7 and 8; seven strips blue stripe 1 1/2" for 9 and 10; eight strips purple/teal

Quilt Specifications

Skill Level: Intermediate
Quilt Size: 62" x 62"
Block Size: Diamond 15" on side
Number of Blocks: 8

Materials

- 1 strip 2 1/2" x 35" medium purple solid for center (C)
- 1/8 yard blue solid for strips 1 and 2
- 1/3 yard light teal solid for strips 3 and 4
- 1/4 yard purple moiré for strips 5 and 6
- 1/2 yard dark teal solid for strips 7 and 8
- 1/3 yard blue stripe for strips 9 and 10
- 2/3 yard purple/teal print for strips 11 and 12
- 1/4 yard black solid for accent strip
- 60" x 60" purple print for background
- 1/3 yard purple/teal print border fabric
- Backing 66" x 66"
- Batting 66" x 66"
- 1 spool matching all-purpose thread
- 1 spool silver metallic thread
- Starmaker 8 tool*
- Binding 61" x 61"
- 6 3/4 yards self-made or purchased binding

Starmaker 8 tool available from Kaye Wood Publishing Co., P.O. Box 456, West Branch, MI 48661 (517) 345-3028.

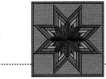

print 2 1/2" for 11 and 12; six strips black solid 1 1/2" for accent strip; and eight strips 1 1/2"-wide purple/teal print border fabric.

Step 2. Sew the center C strips and strip 1 right sides together referring to Figure 1; press seam allowance away from C strip toward strip 1. ***Note:*** *To press, place strip 1 on top, right side down, with C strip underneath right side up. Use the side of the iron (instead of the tip) to press the new strip away from C. The seam allowance will face toward strip 1 and away from C.*

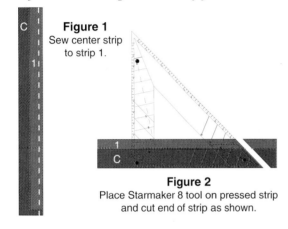

Figure 1
Sew center strip to strip 1.

Figure 2
Place Starmaker 8 tool on pressed strip and cut end of strip as shown.

Step 3. Place the Starmaker 8 tool on the right of the combination strip, with the bottom of the tool lined up with the bottom of the C strips as shown in Figure 2; cut along this angle using a rotary cutter.

Step 4. To measure the distance between cuts, place the 2 1/2" line of a ruler on the cut edge of the strip; butt the Starmaker 8 up against the ruler, keeping the bottom of the tool along the bottom of the C strip as shown in Figure 3. Remove the ruler and cut the second

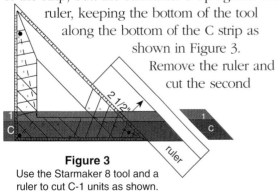

Figure 3
Use the Starmaker 8 tool and a ruler to cut C-1 units as shown.

piece. Cut eight pieces (one for each diamond) from this strip using the tool and the ruler.

Step 5. Start 2" down from the top of strip 2 and sew for about 1" on the right side of just this strip. ***Note:*** *By sewing on just strip 2 for an inch before adding the cut pieces, you anchor the strip; if you start sewing on both the strip and the cut piece at the same time, the angle can become distorted.*

Step 6. Sew a cut piece (C and 1) right side down on strip 2; strip 1 should be at the top and the C piece closest to you as shown in Figure 4. Sew a second cut piece right side down on strip 2, touching but not overlapping the piece already sewn. Continue sewing all eight pieces to strip 2. ***Note:*** *When one strip 2 is not long enough to sew all of the cut pieces needed to it, pick another strip and start sewing pieces to it. Do not sew strips together to make a longer strip.* Press seam allowances toward strip 2 and away from the cut pieces.

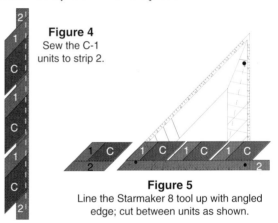

Figure 4
Sew the C-1 units to strip 2.

Figure 5
Line the Starmaker 8 tool up with angled edge; cut between units as shown.

Step 7. Line up the bottom of the Starmaker 8 tool along the bottom of strip 2; line up the side of the tool with the cut edge of strip 1. Cut strip 2 between each piece (C and 1), referring to Figure 5. ***Note:*** *To make it easier to cut if you are right-handed, turn the strip and the tool upside down. Line up the tool with the long strip and the edge of the cut pieces.*

Crystal Star
Placement Diagram
62" x 62"

Step 10. Starting 2" down from the top of strip 4, sew for 1" on the right side of the strip. Sew the C-1-2-3 piece right side down on strip 4 (piece 3 is at the top; piece 1 closest to you) as shown in Figure 8. Sew a second piece right side down on strip 4, touching but not overlapping the piece already sewn. Continue sewing all eight pieces to strip 4; press seam allowances toward strip 4 and away from the cut pieces.

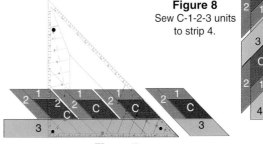

Figure 8
Sew C-1-2-3 units
to strip 4.

Figure 7
Cut segments as shown.

Step 8. Start at the top of strip 3; sew for 1" on the right side of this strip. Sew the cut piece (C, 1 and 2) right side down on strip 3; strip 2 will be at the top and the C piece closest to you as shown in Figure 6. Sew the second cut piece right side down on strip 3, touching but not overlapping the first piece. Continue sewing pieces for all eight diamonds, stopping 3" from the bottom of the strip to allow for the angle cut in the next step; press seam allowances toward strip 3 and away from the cut piece.

Figure 6
Sew C-1-2 unit
to strip 3

Step 9. Line up the bottom of the Starmaker 8 along the bottom of strip 3; line up the side of the tool with the cut edge of C and strip 1. Cut strip 3 between each piece (C, 1 and 2) as shown in Figure 7.

Step 11. Line up the bottom of the Starmaker 8 tool along the bottom of strip 4; line up the side of the tool with the cut edge of piece 3. Cut strip 4 between each piece as shown in Figure 9. **Note:** *Always use two reference points to insure perfect angle—the Starmaker 8 tool along the new strip and the side of the tool along the cut edge of the pieces.*

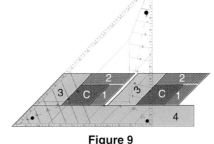

Figure 9
Use tool to cut angle between units as shown.

Figure 10
A completed C-1-2-3-4 unit is shown.

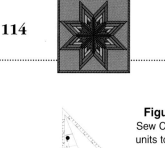
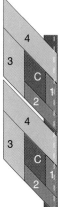

Figure 11
Sew C 1-2-3-4 units to strip 5.

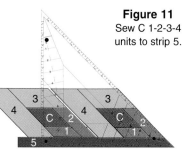

Figure 12
Use tool to cut angle between units.

Step 12. Start at the top of strip 5 and sew for 1" on the right side of the strip. Sew the C-1-2-3-4 pieces right side down on strip 5; piece 4 should be at the top (away from you as you sew); piece 2 will be closest to you. Continue sewing all eight pieces, stopping 3" from the bottom of the strip to allow for the angle cut in the next step. Press the seam allowances toward strip 5 and away from the cut pieces.

Step 13. Line up the bottom of the Starmaker 8 tool along the bottom of strip 5; line up the side of the tool with the cut edge of piece 2. Cut strip 5 between each piece referring to Figure 12 to complete the unit (Figure 13).

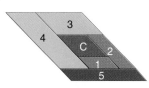

Figure 13
A completed C-1-2-3-4-5 unit is shown.

Step 14. Starting 2" down from the top of strip 6, sew for 1" on the right side of the strip. Sew the C-1-2-3-4-5 units to strip 6 (piece 5 on top; piece 3 closest to you). Continue sewing all eight pieces to strip 6. Press seam allowance

Figure 14
Sew C-1-2-3-4-5 units to strip 6.

toward strip 6 and away from cut pieces. Line up tool as before and cut sections as shown in Figure 15 to make units shown in Figure 16.

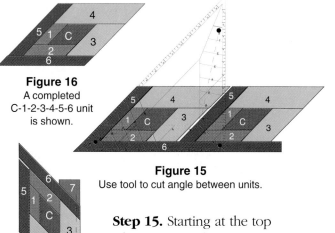

Figure 16
A completed C-1-2-3-4-5-6 unit is shown.

Figure 15
Use tool to cut angle between units.

Step 15. Starting at the top of strip 7, sew for 1" on the right side of the strip. Sew pieced units, right side down, on strip 7 with piece 6 on top and piece 4 closest to you. Continue adding a cut piece for each diamond needed to strip 7, stopping 3" from the bottom of the strip to allow for cutting the angle as shown in Figure 17.

Figure 17
Sew units to strip 7.

Step 16. Line up the bottom of the Starmaker 8 tool on the bottom of strip 7 and the side of the tool with the cut edge of piece 4; cut units as before. **Note:** *Notice how the angle changes direction from one strip to the next, but the last piece added always goes to the top of the strip.* Continue adding strips 8 through 12 in the same manner.

Step 17. To add accent strips, cut strips 1" wide. Sew an accent strip to each strip 11, right sides together, using a 1/4" seam as shown in Figure 19. Fold the strip to the wrong side and press. Stitch in the ditch between strip 11 and the accent strip, from the right side; trim the outside point of the accent strip even with strip 11 as shown in Figure 19.

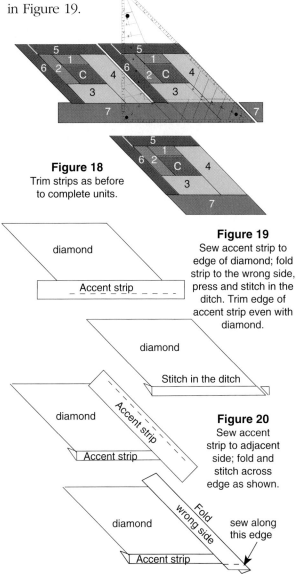

Figure 18
Trim strips as before
to complete units.

Figure 19
Sew accent strip to
edge of diamond; fold
strip to the wrong side,
press and stitch in the
ditch. Trim edge of
accent strip even with
diamond.

Figure 20
Sew accent
strip to adjacent
side; fold and
stitch across
edge as shown.

Step 18. Sew an accent strip to each strip 12. Fold the strip to the wrong side of the diamond; press. To finish the tip, fold the accent strip the opposite way on the pressed fold line with right sides together. Shorten the stitch length; sew the tip of the accent strip about 1/16" along the edge of strip 11 (for turning room) as shown in Figure 20.

Step 19. Trim seam allowance at the point; turn the tip of the accent strip right side out. Press again; stitch in the ditch between the accent strip and strip 12 to finish edge as shown in Figure 21.

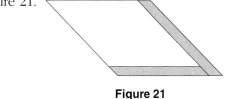

Figure 21
Turn stitched point right side
out to make finished corner
on each star point.

Step 20. Sew four star points together matching seam lines, accent strips and ends; press seam allowances. Join the two star halves together, matching center points (1/8" double-faced basting tape will hold the two points together without pins). Press center seam open.

Step 21. Center the star on the background fabric. Stitch in the ditch in the seam between the accent strip and the star.

Step 22. Add 1 1/2" border strips to each side of background square, mitering corners; trim excess at corners after stitching and press.

Step 23. Prepare quilt for machine quilting referring to Page 156. Machine-quilt using Figure 22 as a guide for stitching.

Step 24. Finish edges referring to Page 157.

Figure 22
Machine-quilt as shown.

By Lynn Graves

Log Cabin Twist

Who says using only solid colors is boring? This fascinating quilt shows how hand-dyed shades of gray combined with hand-dyed solid-color fabrics in a range of colors can create a lively quilt that appears to have movement.

The method of paper piecing used to create the Log Cabin Twist block is very different from the traditional method. In this method, you are sewing on the top of the paper with the lines facing you. The lines are the edge of the fabric piece, not the sewing lines, as in traditional methods.

Because you must sew an exact 1/4" away from these lines, accurate seams are a must. Making even this complicated twisted Log Cabin is simple when you use paper to create extremely accurate designs. A Little Foot gadget helps because it is exactly 1/4" wide; there is no guessing the 1/4" seam allowance; thus less chance for error.

Color is an important part of the design on the quilt, *Isn't Color Wonderful I.* Gradations of color like the ones shown here can only be accomplished by using hand-dyed fabrics. Many fabric shops carry fat-quarter bundles of these fabrics in color families to make it easier for you to find the colors you need.

Have fun creating unusual quilts with this complicated-looking Log Cabin design and a different foundation-piecing technique.

Project Notes

A variety of solid-color fabrics were combined to create the sample quilt which uses over 50 different hand-dyed shades combined with gray. It is recommended that color planning in advance determine the fabrics used. The amount of fabric needed to complete any project will vary with the number of fabrics used.

Play with color before making your fabric

Quilt Specifications
Skill Level: Intermediate
Quilt Size: 30" x 30"
Block Size: 7 1/2" x 7 1/2"
Number of Blocks: 16

Materials
• 1/4 yard each 6 shades of gray
• Various colored scrap strips cut 1 1/2" by the fabric width
• Backing 34" x 34"
• Batting 34" x 34"
• 1 spool matching all-purpose thread
• 1 spool multicolored metallic thread
• Optional: 1 package Log Cabin Twist Foundation Sheets* or photocopy pattern given
• Optional: Little Foot™ presser foot*
For ordering information for Little Foot and Foundation Sheets send LSASE to Little Foot Ltd., 605 Bledsoe, Albuquerque, NM 87107.

choices. Make several enlarged copies of the drawing given in Figure 5 and color using several different choices before deciding on fabrics for your own Log Cabin Twist.

Number the strips on the drawing. Number the fabrics at the selvage of the fabric to correspond to its number in the drawing sequence; or, cut a small piece of fabric and staple to paper and mark with number.

If you are photocopying the pattern, adjust the copier for a very light exposure to minimize the amount of toner on the sheet. The heat of the iron would smear the toner and dirty the bottom of the iron and toner will rub off on the fabric.

Steam-press each strip back and trim along the solid line.

If you do not use a Little Foot, be sure you sew an accurate 1/4" seam allowance from the edge of the presser foot. Use a piece of 1/4" graph paper to check the seam allowance. Sink the needle into the intersection of two squares, lower the presser foot and see where the edge of the foot is in reference to the 1/4" grid. Mark your presser foot with a line at the 1/4" mark using a permanent pen. Use this mark as a guide for matching to lines on the paper.

Set the machine for a very short stitch length to perforate the paper for easy removal. Use a 90/14 needle to make a larger hole in the paper which also makes the paper easier to remove.

Instructions

Note: *In this method of foundation piecing, the fabrics are aligned with the lines on the paper and the stitching is done 1/4" away from the fabrics' edge. The paper is placed with lined side up. In traditional foundation or paper-piecing methods, fabrics are placed on the unmarked side of the paper and stitching is done on the backside on the lines. In the traditional method, the design must be reversed for stitching.*

Step 1. Make 16 copies of the full-size foundation paper given in Figure 1.

Step 2. Cut fabrics into 1 1/2" by fabric width strips.

Step 3. Place strip 1A and 1B on the paper with right sides together. The right edges should be even with the line between 1A and 1B as shown in Figure 2. Position the presser foot as shown on the paper pattern, with the needle exactly 1/4" from the line.

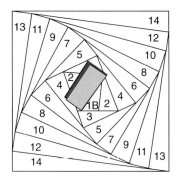

Figure 2
Place first 2 fabric strips on
foundation paper, lining up edges
with line on paper as shown.

Step 4. Begin stitching at the top of 1A, stitching 1/4" from solid line as shown in Figure 3. Exact 1/4" seams are required.

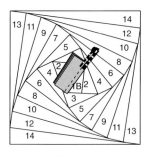

Figure 3
Begin stitching at the top of strip A1.

Step 5. Press piece back; trim edges using the solid line as the guide. Hold the scissors in a cutting position; align the lower blade with the cutting line. Use your other hand to fold the

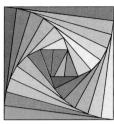

Log Cabin Twist
7 1/2" x 7 1/2" Block

Isn't Color Wonderful I
Placement Diagram
30" x 30"

excess fabric up and over the blade. Cut away excess fabric using the line as a cutting guide as shown in Figure 4. Trim from the point to the base. **Note:** *Because of seam allowance bulk at the intersections, you may wish to grade the seam allowances. Place the strip to be added a tad to the inside edge of the previous strip, but continue to use the solid line as the sewing guide.*

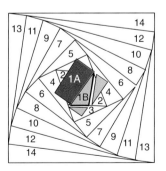

Figure 4
Trim strip even with the line.

Step 6. Align strip 2 facedown with the line between 1A and 2; stitch using a 1/4" seam allowance. Press open; trim as before. Align the opposite 2 strip with the lines between 1B and 2; repeat process. Add strip 3, etc., in the same manner until the block is complete. **Note:** *Do not remove the paper until the quilt top is assembled. If you find it too bulky, remove the paper from the center portion only; leave the outer edges intact for stability.*

Step 7. If a special block arrangement is desired, number each block on the back; draw an arrow pointing to the top of the block to make assembling the top less confusing later.

Step 8. Complete 16 blocks in chosen color arrangement.

Step 9. Arrange the blocks in four rows of four blocks each referring to the Placement Diagram or your own colored diagram for arrangement and using the numbers on the blocks as guides.

Step 10. Join the blocks to form rows; press. Join the rows to complete pieced center; press.

Step 11. Remove all paper from backs of blocks.

Step 12. Sandwich batting between completed top and prepared backing piece. Safety-pin or baste layers together to hold flat.

Step 13. Finish quilt in chosen method referring to Pages 152–160. ***Note:*** *The quilt shown was meander-quilted by machine using metallic thread.*

Figure 5
Enlarge this unfilled drawing and make copies to
experiment with color variations.

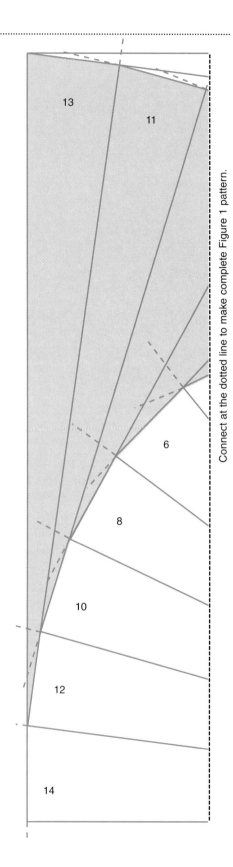

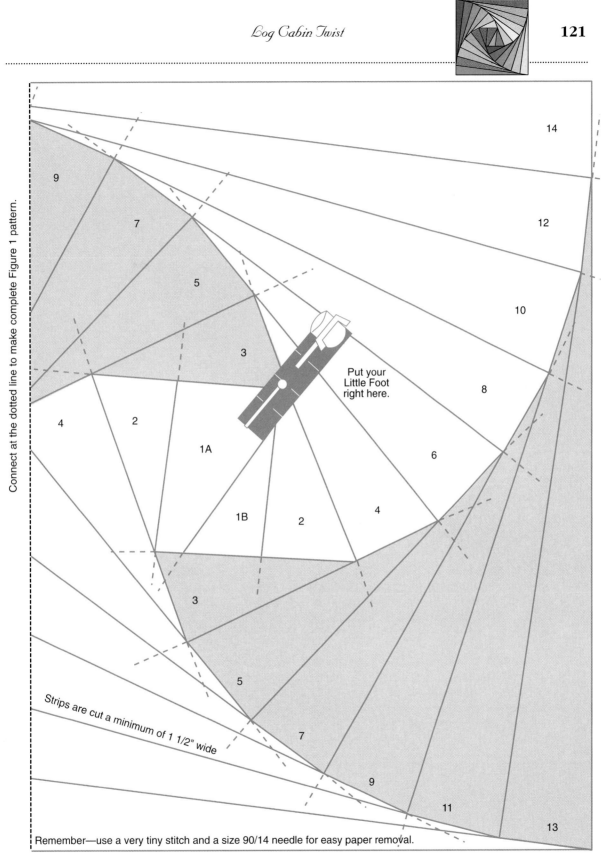

Connect at the dotted line to make complete Figure 1 pattern.

14

9

7

12

5

10

3

Put your
Little Foot
right here.

8

4

2

1A

6

1B

2

4

3

5

Strips are cut a minimum of 1 1/2" wide

7

9

11

13

Remember—use a very tiny stitch and a size 90/14 needle for easy paper removal.

Figure 1
Make 16 copies of this foundation pattern.

By Ann Boyce

Dog Cabin Quilt

It is sometimes hard to find a quilt pattern for a boy's room. This Scottie Dog design, set in the center of a Log Cabin block (thus, Dog Cabin), and made using red, white and blue prints and plaids, is the perfect choice. If you'd like a more feminine look, change the colors to pastels to create a softer feeling.

Making Log Cabin blocks with large center squares creates the perfect place for appliqué shapes. The appliqué should not be done until the blocks are pieced and arranged in rows to assure the correct directional placement of the shapes. When the blocks are all the same, it is easy to determine placement, but when the block forms a pattern determined by different color strips used in the blocks, it is easy to appliqué the shape in the wrong direction.

Dog Cabin is a good example of how a simple design motif can enhance a plain quilt block. Without the dog shapes, the quilt would be rather boring with such large white print centers. Using the same fabric for appliqué shapes as was used in the side and corner triangles ties the whole quilt together for a balanced design.

Instructions

Step 1. Cut the following number of 1 3/4" by fabric width strips from the fabrics listed: five red plaid; seven red print; nine red check; six blue plaid; eight blue print; and nine blue check.

Step 2. Cut three strips 6 1/2" by fabric width white print. Cut each strip into 6 1/2" segments.

Quilt Specifications

Skill Level: Easy
Quilt Size: Approximately 66 3/8" x 66 3/8"
Block Size: 13 1/2" x 13 1/2"
Number of Blocks: 13

Materials

- 1 3/4 yards red/blue/green plaid
- 2/3 yard white print
- 1/3 yard red plaid
- 1/2 yard red print
- 3/4 yard red check
- 1/3 yard blue plaid
- 1/2 yard blue print
- 3/4 yard blue check
- 2 yards blue print for borders
- 1 yard fusible transfer webbing
- Backing 70" x 70"
- Fairfield Processing's Cotton Classic batting 70" x 70"
- 1 spool blue all-purpose thread
- 1 spool transparent nylon thread

You will need 13 of these segments for center squares of blocks.

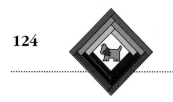
Step 3. Sew white print squares to red plaid strips as shown in Figure 1. Cut strips apart into squares at edge of square; press. Sew these segments to another red plaid strip to add side of first round as shown in Figure 2.

Figure 1
Sew 6 1/2" squares to red plaid strip.

Figure 2
Sew pieced segment to red plaid strip; trim to complete unit.

Step 4. Continue adding segments to strips in this order after the red plaid: blue plaid, blue plaid; red print, red print; blue print, blue print; red check, red check; blue check, blue check. Refer to Figure 3 for color placement.

Figure 3
Sew blocks in color order shown.

Step 5. When all strips have been added and 13 blocks have been completed, trim the blocks to 14" x 14" if necessary; press all seams and trim threads.

Step 6. Cut two squares red/blue/green plaid 20 3/8" x 20 3/8". Cut each square on the diagonal twice to create eight side fill-in triangles as shown in Figure 4.

Step 7. Cut two squares red/blue/green plaid 10 1/2" x 10 1/2". Cut on the diagonal once to create four corner triangles as shown in Figure 5.

Figure 4
Cut 20 3/8" squares on the diagonal twice as shown to make side fill-in triangles.

Figure 5
Cut 10 1/2" squares on the diagonal once for corner triangles.

Step 8. Prepare templates for the dog and bow designs. Fuse the transfer webbing to the wrong side of the red/blue/green plaid. Trace dog and bow designs onto paper side of

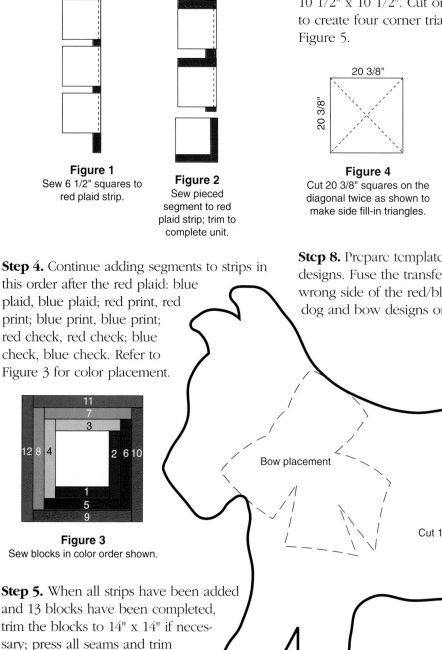

Bow placement

Scottie Dog
Cut 13 red/blue/green plaid

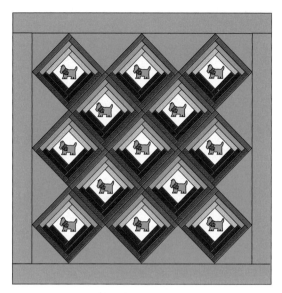

Dog Cabin
Placement Diagram
Approximately 66 3/8" x 66 3/8"

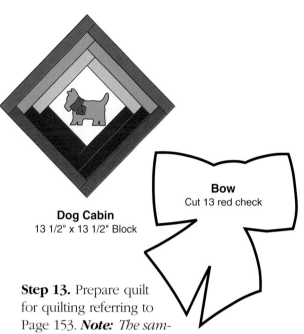

Dog Cabin
13 1/2" x 13 1/2" Block

Bow
Cut 13 red check

fusible, reversing patterns to make dogs face in the direction you want, if necessary.

Step 9. Cut out shapes. Remove paper backing from one dog shape; position in the center of one Log Cabin block with head toward the blue side of the block. Remove paper backing; fuse in place referring to manufacturer's instructions.

Step 10. Machine-appliqué around each shape using transparent nylon thread in the top of the machine and all-purpose thread in the bobbin. Repeat for bow on dog; repeat for all 13 blocks.

Step 11. Arrange the completed blocks in diagonal rows with side fill-in and corner triangles as shown in Figure 6. Join in diagonal rows; join the rows to complete the quilt center; press.

Step 12. Cut two strips blue print 5" x 57 7/8"; sew to two opposite sides of quilt center. Cut two more strips 5" x 66 7/8"; sew a strip to each remaining side; press.

Step 13. Prepare quilt for quilting referring to Page 153. ***Note:*** *The sample quilt shown was machine-quilted in the ditch of the seams of each log, around the appliqué shapes and meander-quilted on the border strips.*

Step 14. Finish edges as desired referring to Pages 157–160. ***Note:*** *The edges on the sample quilt shown were finished by turning the backing to the front and machine-stitching down as directed on Page 157.*

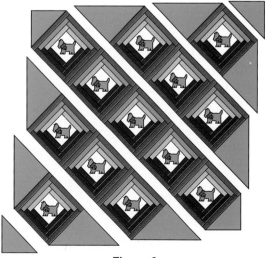

Figure 6
Arrange blocks with corner and side fill-in triangles in diagonal rows as shown.

By Cheryl Fall

Log Cabin Blossoms Baby Quilt

*Flowers are easy to make using a one-sided Log Cabin block.
In this wall hanging designed for a girl's room, the flowers are pieced
using strips with a machine-zigzagged stem. Make this pretty quilt for a
baby or as a summer wall hanging in colors of your choice.*

Like several other projects in this book, the *Log Cabin Blossoms Baby Quilt* is a variation of the traditional Log Cabin block.

Begin with a square and add strips to two sides. The three logs on two sides make up the flower while the wider two logs separate the flower part of the block from the leaf pieces.

Log Cabin blocks are so versatile, and playing with the variations which can be achieved through creative designing is fun. Make this pretty quilt in the colors used or in your favorite flower colors to create your own version of *Log Cabin Blossoms*.

Instructions

Note: *Prewash and press all fabrics. All seam allowances are 1/4" and are included in all measurements given.*

Step 1. Cut nine 3 1/2" x 3 1/2" squares from dark rose print for A.

Step 2. From the assorted 1 1/2" x 44" strips, cut nine pieces of each of the following: B—1 1/2" x 3 1/2"; C—1 1/2" x 4 1/2"; D—1 1/2" x 4 1/2"; E—1 1/2" x 5 1/2"; F—1 1/2" x 5 1/2"; and G—1 1/2" x 6 1/2".

Step 3. Cut nine H pieces 2 1/2" x 6 1/2" and nine I pieces 2 1/2" x 8 1/2" from white solid.

Quilt Specifications

Skill Level: Easy
Quilt Size: 40" x 40"
Block Size: 9" x 9"
Number of Blocks: 9

Materials

- 1 1/4 yards white solid
- 1/4 yard deep rose print
- 1/4 yard light green print
- 1/4 yard dark green print
- Scraps of 6 to 12 assorted fabrics cut in 1 1/2" by fabric width strips (44"), totaling approximately 1 yard
- 4 yards 2 1/2"-wide white pregathered eyelet lace
- 1 spool white Coats Dual-Duty Plus all-purpose thread
- 1 spool green Coats rayon machine embroidery thread
- 1 spool Coats clear nylon monofilament thread
- Backing 44" x 46"
- Batting 44" x 46"

Step 4. Cut nine pieces 1 1/2" x 8 1/2" from dark green for J and nine pieces light green 1 1/2" x 9 1/2" for K.

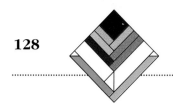

Step 5. To make L pieces, cut nine white solid 1 7/8" x 1 7/8" squares in half on the diagonal to make two triangles from each square for a total of 18 triangles.

Step 6. Referring to Figure 1, sew one of these small triangles to one end of each of the dark green J and light green K strips to make right and left leaf units.

Step 7. Stitch strips B through K to the deep rose squares in alphabetical order referring to Figure 2; press after each addition. Complete nine blocks; press and square blocks up to 9 1/2" x 9 1/2", if necessary.

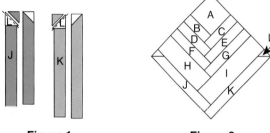

Figure 1
Sew a triangle to the end of each J and K strip; trim off excess.

Figure 2
Sew pieces B through K to the A square in alphabetical order as shown.

Step 8. Cut six 7 1/4" x 7 1/4" squares white solid; cut each square in half on the diagonal to make 12 A triangles as shown in Figure 3.

Step 9. Cut three 14" x 14" squares white solid; cut each square in half on the diagonal twice to make four B triangles from each square for a total of 12 B triangles as shown in Figure 4.

Figure 3
Cut 7 1/4" squares in half on the diagonal to make 12 A triangles.

Figure 4
Cut 14" squares on the diagonal twice to make 12 B triangles.

Step 10. Make one block row by stitching three blocks with four each A and B triangles refer-

ring to Figure 5; press and trim excess white, if necessary. Repeat for three rows.

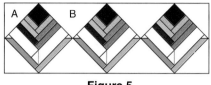

Figure 5
Sew triangles and blocks to make 1 row; repeat for three rows.

Step 11. From the remaining 1 1/2" x 44" strips, cut four 1 1/2" x 38 3/4" C strips and two 1 1/2" x 42 3/4" D strips. Join the block rows with the C strips, starting and ending with a strip; press.

Step 12. Sew the D strips to the long sides, referring to Figure 6; press.

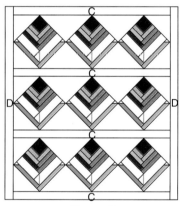

Figure 6
Sew rows with C strips; add D strips to sides.

Step 13. Hand-baste the batting to the wrong side of the quilt top. Machine-baste close to the raw edges; trim away excess batting.

Step 14. Baste the eyelet lace around the edges of the quilt top. Place the quilt top and backing piece right sides together; pin layers together to hold.

Step 15. Stitch around all four sides, leaving a 10" opening along one edge for turning. Trim edges even, clip corners and turn right side out

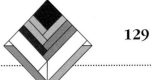

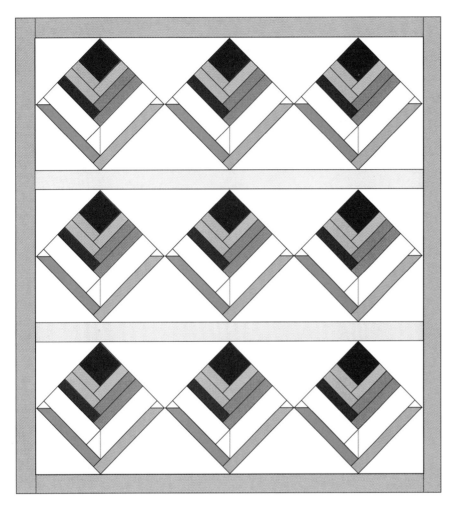

Log Cabin Blossoms
9" x 9" Block

Log Cabin Blossoms
Placement Diagram
40 1/4" x 42 1/4" (without lace)

through the opening. Hand-stitch the opening closed.

Step 16. Remove the basting stitches. Pin-baste the three layers together; machine-quilt as desired using the clear nylon monofilament in the top of the machine and all-purpose thread in the bobbin.

Step 17. Machine satin-stitch the stem lines in place using the green rayon thread and a medium-width zigzag stitch to complete.

By Beth Wheeler

Rock-a-Bye Baby

For an interesting twist on the traditional Log Cabin block try our crib quilt with a rotated axis. If you prefer a less feminine quilt, use darker colors and no ruffle to create a quilt with a totally different look.

Make traditional blocks with a wider outside round and trim to an off-center axis to create this pretty pastel-colored baby quilt.

Have some fun with the leftover pieces by using them in a pieced border. Don't worry if all sides aren't exactly the same—this is a child's quilt, after all! Strip-piece the strips left over from piecing the blocks and create long strips which are trimmed to size after stitching.

If you want to try to make all sides equal, center the strip and pin to sides, working from the center to the corners. This should result in an equal amount of fabric left on each end. Short of cutting perfect templates and sewing pieces together one at a time (too time-consuming), this is the best way to use up the scraps and add an interesting border at the same time.

Instructions

Step 1. Cut strips the width of each light pastel fabric in the following widths: three 1 3/4" and four 2 1/2". Cut four 1 3/4" and four 2 1/2" strips from each dark pastel fabric. Place beside sewing machine within easy reach. Cut one 12" piece from one 1 3/4" strip of each fabric.

Step 2. Place one 12" strip light pastel on top of one 12" strip coordinating dark pastel with right sides facing; stitch. Press seam allowance

Quilt Specifications
Skill Level: Intermediate
Quilt Size: 52" x 60" (without ruffle)
Block Size: 8" x 8"
Number of Blocks: 30

Materials
• 1/2 yard each of 5 light pastel fabrics
• 1/2 yard each of 5 deep pastel fabrics to coordinate with light pastel fabrics
• 4 yards pink check (borders and ruffle)
• Fairfield Processing's Feather Touch cotton batting 56" x 64"
• Backing 56" x 64"
• 1 spool neutral sewing thread
• 1 spool lightweight monofilament thread
• 1 sheet clear plastic template material
• 1 black permanent pen

toward lighter log, being careful not to distort fabric.

Step 3. Cut stitched strip into six 1 3/4" units, as shown in Figure 1. Stack in a pile, right side down and with light pastel at the top.

Step 4. Place another 1 3/4" dark pastel strip on the sewing machine bed. Place one unit

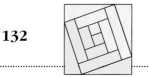
from stack on top, with right sides facing, as shown in Figure 2. Stitch along long edge of strips, placing another unit next to the first one until all units are used. Press all seam allowances away from center log.

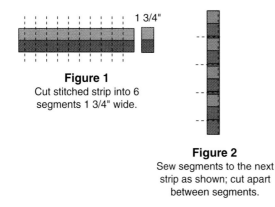

Figure 1
Cut stitched strip into 6
segments 1 3/4" wide.

Figure 2
Sew segments to the next
strip as shown; cut apart
between segments.

Step 5. Cut strips apart between units. Open; press seam allowance away from center. Stack right side down, with last strip added at top referring to Figure 3.

Step 6. Place a 1 3/4" dark pastel strip on sewing machine bed. Place a stitched unit on top, with right sides facing, as shown in Figure 4. Stitch along long edge, placing another next to first one, until all units are used. Use another dark pastel strip if necessary to complete round on all segments.

Step 7. Repeat with two light pastel strips. The

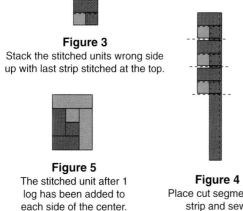

Figure 3
Stack the stitched units wrong side
up with last strip stitched at the top.

Figure 5
The stitched unit after 1
log has been added to
each side of the center.

Figure 4
Place cut segment on
strip and sew.

pieced segment should now look like Figure 5. Stitch one round of two dark pastel logs and two light pastel logs. Always apply light pastel log to light pastel side of block and dark pastel log to dark pastel side of block. The final round is stitched with 2 1/2" strips as shown in Figure 6.

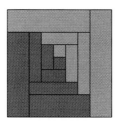

Figure 6
The completed unit is shown.

Step 8. Repeat with other pairs of pastel fabrics for six blocks of each color (30 total).

Stitching

Step 1. Place clear plastic over pattern given in Figure 7 on Pages 122 and 123. Trace all marks with permanent marker; add 1/4" all around for seam allowance before cutting out.

Step 2. Center template on one block, matching marks with seams. Cut around template; repeat for remaining blocks.

Step 3. Arrange blocks in six rows of five blocks each referring to the Placement Diagram. Join blocks in rows; press seam allowances in one direction. Join the rows; press.

Step 4. Stitch remaining fabric strips together along long sides for pieced border. Press seam allowances in one direction. Cut strips into 2" segments. Join along short ends to make two strips with 34 units and two strips with at least 31 units.

Step 5. Cut two each 2" x 48 1/2" and 2" x 43 1/2" strips pink check for first border and

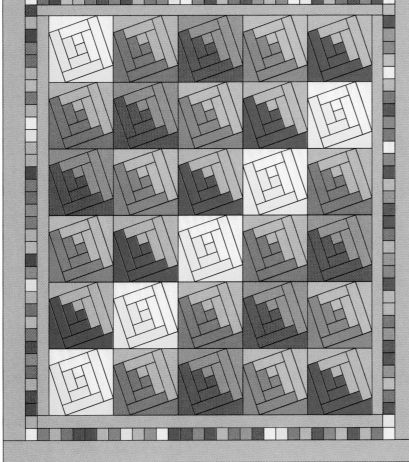

Rock-a-Bye Baby Log
8" x 8" Block

Rock-a-Bye Baby
Placement Diagram
52" x 60" (without ruffle)

two each 3 1/2" x 54 1/2" and 3 1/2" x 52 1/2" strips pink check for third border.

Step 6. Stitch one 2" x 48 1/2" pink check strip on each long side of the quilt center; press seam allowances toward strips. Stitch remaining 2" x 43 1/2" strips to the top and bottom; press seam allowances toward strips.

Step 7. Stitch one pieced strip with 34 units along each long side; press and trim excess.

Sew the strips with 31 units along the top and bottom. **Note:** *The strip should be a bit too long. Center each strip before sewing. Cut off an equal amount from each end after stitching.* Press and trim excess at each end.

Step 8. Stitch a 3 1/2" x 54 1/2" strip to each side; press seam toward strip. Sew a 3 1/2" x 52 1/2" strip to the top and bottom; press seam toward strip.

Ruffle

Step 1. Cut 10 pink check strips 6 1/2" by fabric width for ruffle. Join the strips on short ends to make one long strip.

Step 2. Fold strip in half lengthwise; press.

Step 3. Run a gathering stitch along raw edge with sewing machine.

Step 4. Pin ruffle along raw edge of right side of quilt top, adjusting ruffles evenly around outside edge and allowing extra fullness to turn corners without cupping.

Step 5. Stitch through ruffle and quilt top with a 1/4" seam allowance.

Finishing

Step 1. Place quilt top on work surface, right side up. Position prepared quilt back on top; smooth gently to remove wrinkles without stretching. Trim backing to match quilt top.

Step 3. Place batting on quilt back. Smooth gently from center outward to remove wrinkles without stretching batting; trim evenly with quilt top. Pin in place around outside edges.

Step 4. Stitch with a 1/4" seam allowance all around outside edges, leaving a 4" opening for turning.

Step 5. Clip corners; turn right side out. Hand-stitch opening closed.

Step 6. Quilt 1/4" away from edge, through all seams and as desired over quilt's surface.

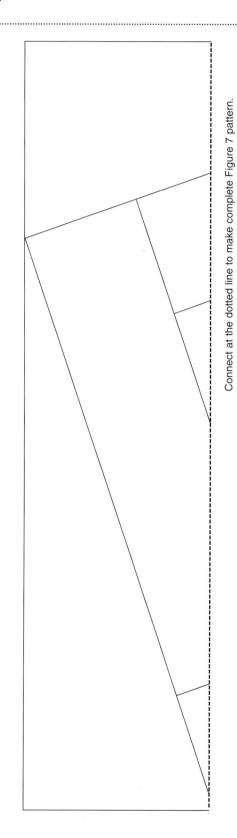

Connect at the dotted line to make complete Figure 7 pattern.

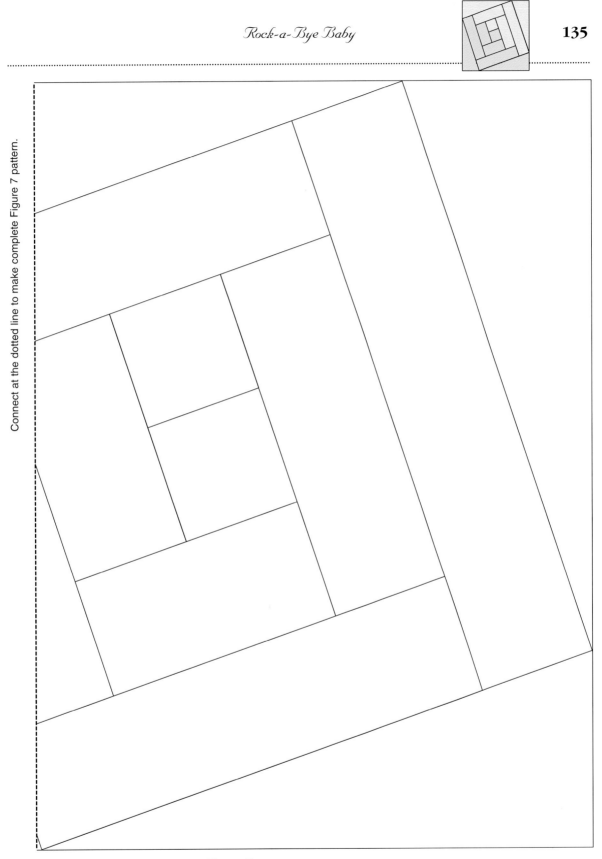

Connect at the dotted line to make complete Figure 7 pattern.

Figure 7
Full-size block drawing. Add 1/4" seam allowance all around when cutting.

By Connie Rand

Log Cabin in the Woods

As I sat down at my computer to play with Log Cabin blocks, I decided to use the blocks to make a picture. The name of the block suggested that I try to build a log cabin. It seemed to me that the cabin should be in a wooded setting, so I added the spruces around the cabin. Scrap fabrics were used to make the scene come alive.

Because the design I created was horizontal, and didn't seem suited to use on a bed, I decided to use small blocks to make a wall hanging. The blocks were so small that paper piecing proved to be the easiest way to handle the tiny strips needed to construct the blocks. For detailed instructions on paper piecing, see Page 150.

Some of the blocks used in the quilt are made of one color and some combine two colors. Refer to Figure 1 for color combinations and the number of blocks to make in each combination.

Even though the blocks are very small and the finished width of the strips is only 1/4", using paper-piecing methods creates perfectly accurate blocks making this an easy, but time-consuming project.

Instructions

Step 1. Cut two strips brown print 1 3/4" x 33 1/2" and two strips 1 3/4" x 22 1/4". Set aside for borders. Cut 3/4" strips from each of the fabrics except green border print.

Step 2. Make 84 copies of the full-size paper-piecing drawing shown in Figure 2. Referring to Figure 1, use colored pencils to color the drawings to help with placement of colors on each

Quilt Specifications
Skill Level: Intermediate
Quilt Size: 27 3/4" x 41 1/2"
Block Size: 2 3/4" x 2 3/4"
Number of Blocks: 84

Materials
• 1/4 yard total red print scraps
• 1/4 yard total yellow print scraps
• 1 yard total brown print scraps
• 1 1/2 yards total green print scraps
• 1 1/2 yards total blue print scraps
• 1 yard green print for borders
• Backing 31" x 45"
• Batting 31" x 45"
• All-purpose thread to match fabrics
• 4 yards self-made or purchased binding

block. ***Note:*** *The blue/green blocks have two blue squares in the center of the block, while the blue/brown and red/brown blocks have one square of each color in the center. I wanted the trees to have a rougher look, and chose to put two blue squares in the center to interrupt the silhouette of the tree branches.*

Step 3. Sew chosen center color strips together as shown in Figure 3; press seam toward darker fabric. Cut apart at 3/4" intervals. The resulting segments will be used as centers on the paper foundation pieces.

Step 4. Sew pieces to paper foundations in numerical order referring to Page 150 for instructions and to Figure 1 for color combinations and number of blocks needed in each combination.

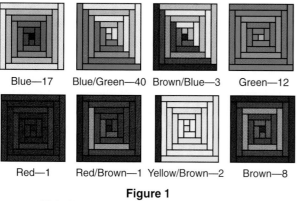

Figure 1

Make blocks in color combinations and number shown. Each block finishes at 2 3/4".

Blue—17   Blue/Green—40   Brown/Blue—3   Green—12
Red—1   Red/Brown—1   Yellow/Brown—2   Brown—8

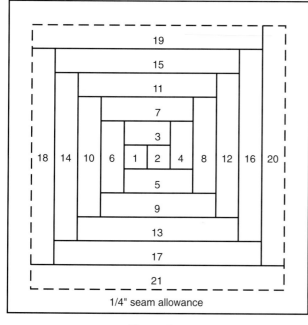

1/4" seam allowance

Figure 2

Make 84 copies of this full-size paper-piecing diagram. Color your copies to match blocks in Figure 1.

Step 5. Complete 84 blocks; press carefully; trim all loose threads and cut blocks to 3 1/4" x 3 1/4" if necessary. ***Note:*** *Leave the paper in place until after rows are stitched.*

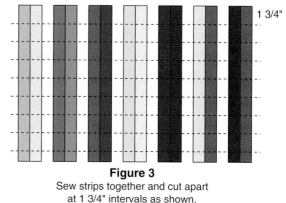

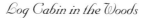

1 3/4"

Figure 3

Sew strips together and cut apart at 1 3/4" intervals as shown.

Step 6. Arrange the blocks in rows referring to Figure 4; join the blocks in rows. Join the rows; trim threads and press joining seams carefully.

Step 7. Remove paper from behind each block.

Step 8. Sew the 1 3/4" x 33 1/2" brown print strips to the top and bottom. Sew the 1 3/4" x 22 1/4" brown print strips to the sides; press seams toward brown print.

Step 9. Cut two strips green border print 3 1/2" x 36"; sew to top and bottom. Cut two more strips green print 3 1/2" x 28 1/4"; sew to sides. Press seams toward green print.

Step 10. Prepare quilt for quilting referring to Page 155. ***Note:*** *The sample shown was machine-quilted. Because there are so many seams, quilting was done only around each block in the ditch of the seams.*

Step 11. Finish edges with self-made or purchased binding as directed on Page 157 to finish.

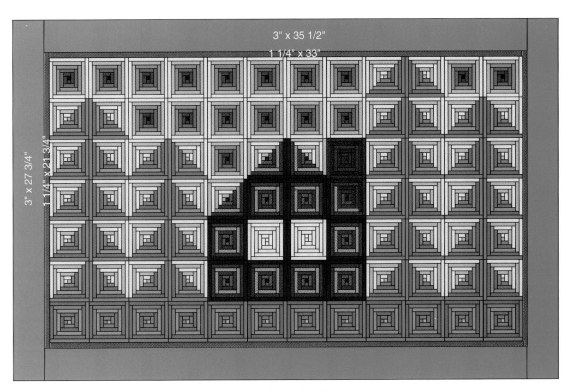

Log Cabin in the Woods
Placement Diagram
27 3/4" x 41 1/2"

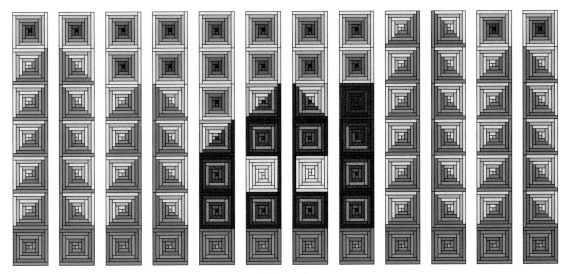

Figure 4
Sew blocks together in rows as shown.

By Wanda S. Hanson

Crazy Logs

Instead of giving you specific instructions for a quilt, I am sharing general instructions for a method that works for me. I love making crazy Log Cabin-type blocks using scraps of all colors.

Even though the Log Cabin blocks in the quilt shown here are pieced in a crazy-block method, you can still tell they are Log Cabins. They begin in the center and work from side to side in a Courthouse Steps fashion using irregular shapes and strip widths.

There is no right or wrong color, no right or wrong size, no accuracy and no stress. Each block is pieced until it feels done. The only exact size you need is when you are ready to join the blocks. In most quilts, all blocks must be the same size. In the quilt shown, two blocks are one size and two another so there is not a center where all four meet exactly!

Unlike regular Log Cabin methods where there is an even number of logs on each side, I just continue to piece using as many strips as needed to reach the desired size. The pieces near the outside edge of the blocks are usually wider than the center strips.

I feel very free and relaxed when making my crazy Log Cabin blocks. There are no restrictions or rules and no preplanning. I just reach for a color as I decide it is needed. The sewing table is a mess when I finish because I like to work with a large variety of fabrics and repeat colors rather than repeating the same fabric. When I clean up all of the leftovers, I some-

Quilt Specifications

Skill Level: Easy
Quilt Size: Any size
Block Size: Any size
Number of Blocks: Any number

Materials

- Scraps in any size and shape with smaller pieces used in the center area and longer strip scraps needed for the outer edges
- Batting and backing 4" larger than quilt top all around
- All-purpose thread to match fabrics

times piece tiny crazy blocks rather than throw away the little scraps. They become Christmas tree ornaments or gifts.

If you are tired of the exacting nature of most pieced and appliqué quilts, you will love making *Crazy Logs*!

Instructions

Step 1. You may work with or without foundation paper or fabric. If using paper or fabric, cut to size larger than the finished block size. Mark the center. To make a block, choose the piece of fabric for the center. Choose the piece which will go next to it. Place on paper or fabric foundation right sides together and sew as shown in Figure 1.

Step 2. If not using foundation methods, sew the center piece and the next fabric strip to it as shown in Figure 2. Finger-press seam and add next piece as if you were making a normal Log Cabin block except don't worry about shape.

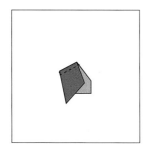

Figure 1
Sew an irregular-size strip to center shape on foundation as shown.

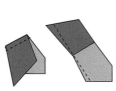

Figure 2
Sew 2 pieces of fabric together as shown. Press and trim to shape if necessary.

Step 3. Continue adding strips around center in desired order (whether using foundation or traditional sewing methods) until block is desired size. Trim to exact size, adding 1/2" for seam allowance as shown in Figure 3.

Figure 3
Trim finished block to any size.

Step 4. Complete the desired number of blocks needed to make the size quilt you have planned.

Step 5. Lay the blocks out to find a pleasing arrangement. Join the blocks in rows; join the rows to complete the top.

Step 6. Borders may be added to frame the blocks, or sashing strips may be used to separate the blocks. In the quilt shown a narrow black border was used to contain the center area and relates well to the black-and-white print outer border. The chosen binding fabric picks up some of the brilliant pink areas within the pieced area.

Step 7. Finish the quilt as desired referring to Pages 152–160.

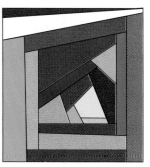

Crazy Log Cabin
Any Size Block

Tips & Techniques

If you have no scraps (we can't imagine it, but just in case!), work with 3" strips. Keep angling each new strip as it is sewn to achieve an irregular-shaped block. Combine all types of prints and fabrics to create texture as well as design. Sometimes blocks may be pieced over an extended period of time to be saved until enough blocks have been constructed to make the desired-size quilt. To tie all the blocks together, one fabric might be repeated in each block.

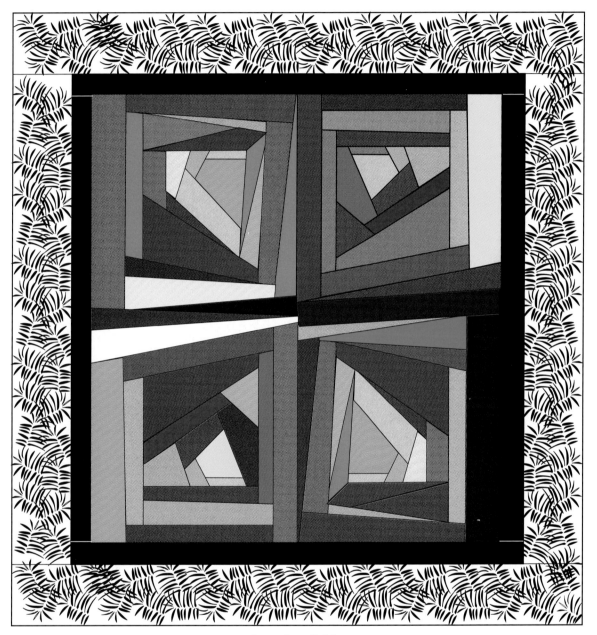

Crazy Log Cabin
Placement Diagram
Any Size

Log Cabin Basics

Materials & Supplies

Fabrics

Fabric Choices. Log Cabin quilts are beautiful whether you choose to make them from all new, specially purchased fabrics, use scraps or a combination of both. Many of the Log Cabin quilts in this book use scraps for the logs. They may be in one color family, all dark or all light. Because most Log Cabin designs are formed by the placement of lights and darks, sometimes the value—not the color—is most important.

Antique quilts used scraps which sometimes were pieced together to make a piece large enough to use (see Page ??). Today most of us use scraps from leftover projects, not from old clothes. Still, using our scraps is important to us.

Buying Fabrics. One hundred percent cotton fabrics are recommended for making quilts. Choose colors similar to those used in the quilts shown or colors of your own preference. Most Log Cabin quilt designs depend more on contrast of values than on the colors used to create the design.

Preparing the Fabric for Use. Fabrics may be prewashed or not depending on your preference. Whether you prewash or not, be sure your fabrics are colorfast and won't run onto each other when washed after use.

Fabric Grain. Fabrics are woven with threads going in a crosswise and lengthwise direction. The threads cross at right angles—the more threads per inch, the stronger the fabric.

The crosswise threads will stretch a little. The lengthwise threads will not stretch at all. Cutting the fabric at a 45-degree angle to the crosswise and lengthwise threads produces a bias edge which stretches a great deal when pulled (Figure 1).

Most patterns in this book do not require templates. Instead they use strips of fabric which are cut crosswise to the fabric grain. If a template is given, pay careful attention to the grain lines marked with arrows. These arrows indicate that the piece should be placed on the lengthwise grain with the arrow running on one thread. Although it is not necessary to examine the fabric and find a thread to match to, it is important to try to place the arrow with the lengthwise grain of the fabric (Figure 2).

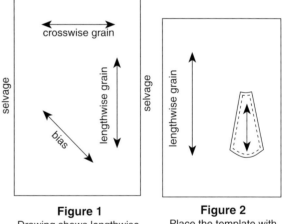

Figure 1
Drawing shows lengthwise, crosswise and bias threads.

Figure 2
Place the template with marked arrow on the lengthwise grain of the fabric.

Thread

For most piecing, good-quality cotton or cotton-covered polyester is the thread of choice. Inexpensive polyester threads are not recommended because they can cut the fibers of cotton fabrics.

Choose a color thread that will match or blend

with the fabrics in your quilt. Most Log Cabin quilts are pieced with dark and light color fabrics. Choose a neutral thread color, such as a medium gray, as a compromise between colors. Test by pulling a sample seam.

Batting

Batting is the material used to give a quilt loft or thickness. It also adds warmth. Many antique Log Cabin quilts were pieced on foundations and used no extra filling between the top and the backing. Some of these quilts used flannel as the foundation, thus adding extra warmth with this layer.

Batting size is listed in inches for each pattern to reflect the size needed to complete the quilt according to the instructions. Purchase the size large enough to cut the size you need for the quilt of your choice.

Qualities to look for in batting are drapeability, resistance to fiber migration, loft and softness.

If you are unsure which kind of batting to use, purchase the smallest size batting available in the type you'd like to try. Test each sample on a small project. Choose the batting that you like working with most and that will result in the type of quilt you need.

Templates

Templates should be accurate and marked with the pattern name and piece number or letter to identify it should it be separated from the rest of the pattern at a later date (Figure 3).

Figure 3
Mark each template with the pattern name and piece indentification.

Tools & Equipment

There are few truly essential tools and little equipment required for quiltmaking. The basics include needles (hand-sewing and quilting betweens), pins (long, thin sharp pins are best), sharp scissors or shears, a thimble, template materials (plastic or cardboard), marking tools (chalk marker, water-erasable pen and a No. 2 pencil are a few) and a quilting frame or hoop. For piecing and/or quilting by machine, add a sewing machine to the list.

Sewing basics such as a seam ripper, pincushion, measuring tape and an iron are also necessary. For choosing colors or quilting designs for your quilt, or for designing your own quilt, it is helpful to have graph paper, tracing paper, colored pencils or markers and a ruler.

For making Log Cabin quilts, a rotary cutter, mat and specialty rulers are a must. We recommend an ergonomic rotary cutter, a large self-healing mat and several rulers. If you can choose only one size, a 6" x 24" marked in 1/8" or 1/4" increments is recommended.

Construction Methods

Traditional Templates. While most instructions in this book use rotary-cut strips and quick sewing methods, several patterns require a template. Templates are like pattern pieces used to sew a garment. They are used to cut the fabric pieces which make up the quilt top. There are two types—templates that include a 1/4" seam allowance and those that don't.

Choose the template material and the pattern. Transfer the pattern shapes to the template material with a sharp No. 2 lead pencil. Write the pattern name, piece letter or number, grain line and number to cut for one block (whole quilt) on each piece.

Some patterns (see *Santa's Log Cabin* on Page 99) require a reversed piece (Figure 4). These patterns are labeled with an R after the piece letter; for example, B and BR. To reverse a template, first cut it with the labeled side up and then with the labeled side down. Compare these to the right and left fronts of a blouse. When making a garment, you accomplish reversed pieces when cutting the pattern on two layers of fabric placed with right sides together. This can be done when cutting templates as well.

If cutting one layer of fabric at a time, first trace the template onto the backside of the fabric with the marked side down; turn the template over with the marked side on the top to make reverse pieces.

Figure 4
This pattern uses reversed pieces.

Hand-Piecing Basics. When hand-piecing it is easier to begin with templates which do not include the 1/4" seam allowance. Place the template on the wrong side of the fabric, lining up the marked grain line with lengthwise or crosswise fabric grain. If the piece does not have to be reversed, place with labeled side up. Trace around shape; move, leaving 1/2" between the shapes, and mark again.

When you have marked the appropriate number of pieces, cut out pieces, leaving 1/4" beyond marked line all around each piece.

Patterns in this book include a drawing suggesting the assembly order. Refer to these drawings to piece units and blocks.

To join two units, place the patches with right sides together. Stick a pin in at the beginning of the seam through both fabric patches, matching the beginning points (Figure 5); for hand-piec-

Figure 5
Stick a pin through fabrics to match the beginning of the seam.

Figure 6
Begin hand-piecing at seam, not at the edge of the fabric. Continue stitching along seam line.

ing, the seam begins on the traced line, not at the edge of the fabric (see Figure 6).

Thread a sharp needle; knot one strand of the thread at the end. Remove the pin and insert the needle in the hole; make a short stitch and then a backstitch right over the first stitch. Continue making short stitches with several stitches on the needle at one time. As you stitch, check the back piece often to assure accurate stitching on the seam line. Take a stitch at the end of the seam; backstitch and knot at the same time as shown in Figure 7.

Seams on hand-pieced fabric patches may be finger-pressed toward the darker fabric.

To sew units together, pin fabric patches together, matching seams. Sew as above except where seams meet; at these intersections, backstitch, go through seam to next piece and backstitch again to secure seam joint.

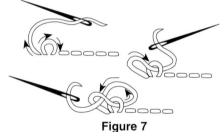

Figure 7
Make a loop in a backstitch to make a knot.

All pieced blocks can't be stitched with straight seams or in rows. Some patterns, like a star, require set-in pieces. To begin a set-in seam, pin one side of the square to the proper side of the star point with right sides together, matching corners. Start stitching at the seam line on the outside point; stitch on the marked seam line to the end of the seam line at the center referring to Figure 8.

Bring around the adjacent side and pin to the next star point, matching seams. Continue the stitching line from the adjacent seam through corners and to the outside edge of the square as shown in Figure 9.

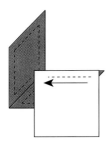
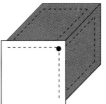

Figure 8
To set a square into a diamond point, match seams and stitch from outside edge to center.

Figure 9
Continue stitching the adjacent side of the square to the next diamond shape in 1 seam from center to outside as shown.

Machine-Piecing. If making templates, include the 1/4" seam allowance on the template for machine-piecing. Place template on the wrong side of the fabric as for hand-piecing except butt pieces against one another when tracing.

Set machine on 2.5 or 12–15 stitches per inch. Join pieces as for hand-piecing for set-in seams; but for other straight seams, begin and end sewing at the end of the fabric patch sewn as shown in Figure 10. No backstitching is necessary when machine-stitching.

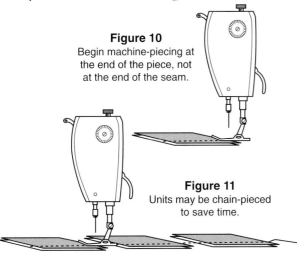

Figure 10
Begin machine-piecing at the end of the piece, not at the end of the seam.

Figure 11
Units may be chain-pieced to save time.

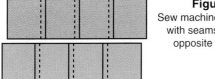

Figure 12
Sew machine-pieced units with seams pressed in opposite directions.

Join units as for hand-piecing referring to the piecing diagrams where needed. Chain piecing (Figure 11—sewing several like units before sewing other units) saves time by eliminating beginning and ending stitches and is used for most Log Cabin strip sewing.

When joining machine-pieced units, match seams against each other with seam allowances pressed in opposite directions to reduce bulk and make perfect matching of seams possible (Figure 12).

Quick-Cutting. Quick-cutting and piecing strips is recommended for making Log Cabin quilts. Templates are completely eliminated; instead, a rotary cutter, plastic ruler and mat are used to cut fabric logs.

When rotary-cutting strips, straighten raw edges of fabric by folding fabric in fourths across the width as shown in Figure 13. Press down flat; place ruler on fabric square with edge of fabric and make one cut from the folded edge to the outside edge. If strips are not straightened, a wavy strip will result as shown in Figure 14.

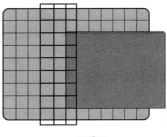

Figure 13
Fold fabric and straighten as shown.

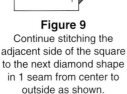

Figure 14
Wavy strips result if fabric is not straightened before cutting.

Always cut away from your body, holding the ruler firmly with the non-cutting hand. Keep fingers away from the edge of the ruler as it is easy for the rotary cutter to slip and jump over the edge of the ruler if cutting is not properly done.

Log Cabin piecing begins in the center of the block, and logs are added in rounds. The center piece may be the same width as the logs, or it may be larger, smaller or a different shape; it depends on the patterns you choose. If it is a square, it can be sub-cut from a strip as shown in Figure 15.

If two same-size pieces are used in the center, sew two proper-width strips together and cut both centers at the same time (Figure 16).

It would be difficult to list the number of cut strips needed of each chosen fabric. Figure it out yourself by taking the length of the log (plus seams) and dividing that number into the width of the fabric you are cutting. If you are cutting on the crosswise grain of the fabric, that would probably be 44" or 45".

For example, if the log needed was 1 1/2" x 6 1/2", cut fabric strips 1 1/2" across the width of the fabric. Dividing 44" by 6 1/2" tells you that you can get six full logs with some left over from each strip. If you have 20 blocks using this 6 1/2" strip, divide 20 by 6. The number of strips needed is an uneven number so you need the next highest number of strips, which in this case is four, to make that log.

If you are using strips cut on the lengthwise grain of the fabric, the length is whatever yardage you have. After you find out how many strips you can cut from that length, repeat the dividing process to figure out the number of strips needed. The outer logs are longer with fewer logs being cut from each strip; therefore, the outer strips require more fabric than the inner strips.

If you need triangles, you can use the same method, but you need to figure out how wide to cut the strip. Measure the finished size of one side of the triangle. Add 7/8" to this size for seam allowance. Cut fabric strips this width; cut the strips into the same increment to create squares. Cut the squares on the diagonal to produce triangles. For example, if you need a triangle with a 2" finished height, cut the strips 2 7/8" by the width of the fabric. Cut the strips into 2 7/8" squares. Cut each square on the diagonal to produce the correct-size triangle (Figure 17).

Triangles sewn together to make squares are called half-square triangles or triangle/squares. When squares are cut on the diagonal to make these triangles, the straight of grain is on the two short sides, not the diagonal. When joined, the triangle/square unit has the straight of grain on all outside edges of the block.

Half-square triangles are used to make many designs. See the *Log Cabin for Christmas* on Page 95 for an example of a quilt that could be made using these quick methods instead of templates.

If you need triangles with the straight of grain on the diagonal, such as for fill-in triangles on the outside edges of a diagonal-set quilt, the procedure is a bit different.

To make these triangles, a square is cut on both diagonals; thus, the straight of grain is on the longest or diagonal side (Figure 18). To figure

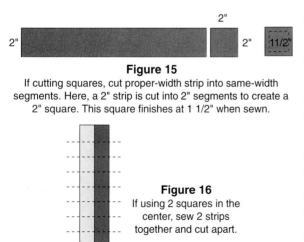

Figure 15
If cutting squares, cut proper-width strip into same-width segments. Here, a 2" strip is cut into 2" segments to create a 2" square. This square finishes at 1 1/2" when sewn.

Figure 16
If using 2 squares in the center, sew 2 strips together and cut apart.

out the size to cut the square, add 1 1/4" to the needed finished size of the longest side of the triangle. For example, if you need a triangle with a 12" finished diagonal, cut a 13 1/4" square.

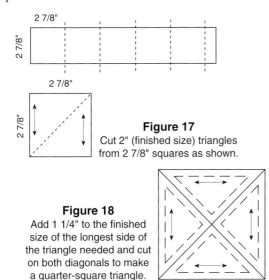

Figure 17
Cut 2" (finished size) triangles from 2 7/8" squares as shown.

Figure 18
Add 1 1/4" to the finished size of the longest side of the triangle needed and cut on both diagonals to make a quarter-square triangle.

If templates are given, use their measurements to cut fabric strips that correspond with that measurement. Then use the template on the strip to cut pieces quickly. Strip cutting works best for squares, triangles, rectangles and diamonds. Odd-shaped templates are difficult to cut in multiple layers or using a rotary cutter.

Tips & Techniques

Quilts with blocks set on the diagonal often use plain blocks between pieced blocks and plain corner and fill-in triangles. These all may be cut using a rotary cutter and faster methods as described. Notice that the quarter-square fill-in triangles have the straight of grain on the outside edges and the corner triangles have the straight of grain on both sides. The general rule is to keep the outside edges of blocks on quilts on the straight of grain. This will reduce stretching during the finishing processes and keep the quilt square (Figure 19).

Quick-Piecing Method. After the strips have been cut, you are ready to sew. Set machine at 2.5 or 12–15 stitches per inch. Lay one center unit on the first log strip under the presser foot of the sewing machine right sides together. Sew an exact 1/4" seam allowance to the end of the square; place another square right next to the first one and continue sewing, adding a square after every stitched square, until all of the center squares are used up (Figure 20).

When sewing is finished, press seam away from center from right side of strip, using the tip of your iron. Cut apart as shown in Figure 21 using your rotary cutter and a straight edge again.

To make strips circle around the center in a clockwise direction, turn pieces in a counter-clockwise direction when sewing. Stack the blocks to the left of the sewing machine, right side down, with the last strip sewn away from you toward the back of the machine. When you pick up the blocks to place on the next strip, they are in the exact position for placement on the strip. Repeat the same procedure again. ***Note:*** *It is easy to make a mistake and sew the strip to the wrong side of the log block. Check the first addition to make sure you are adding the strip on the proper side of the block.*

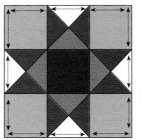

Figure 19
Notice that with properly cut pieces, the straight of grain is always on the outside edge of the quilt.

Continue adding strips as shown in Figure 22, pressing and cutting until you have enough logs on the block. You may need to cut more strips if you did not calculate accurately in the beginning.

Save time by working on the same strip on all blocks rather than one block at a time. When you get closer to the edge, it takes longer to finish the blocks because the strips are so much longer than they were in the beginning.

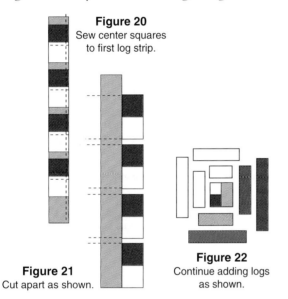

Figure 20
Sew center squares to first log strip.

Figure 21
Cut apart as shown.

Figure 22
Continue adding logs as shown.

Quilt-as-You-Stitch. Another method is to complete the blocks and quilting all in one step. Cut batting and backing the size of the finished block plus 1/2". Baste batting to wrong side of backing square.

Starting with the center squares, stitch strips or log pieces directly onto the batting in the same manner as speed-piecing as shown in Figure 23.

Stop stitching 1/4" from edge on strips along outside edge as shown in Figure 24. Trim the batting to the finished size of the block. Join the blocks together by sewing the top fabric only (do not catch batting in seam), joining blocks in rows and then joining rows. Turn under a 1/4"

seam allowance on all edges of the backing; stitch backing squares together by hand.

Figure 23
Sew strips to batting squares, starting in the center as shown.

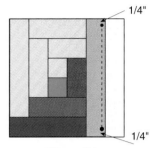

Figure 24
Stop stitching on outside strips 1/4" from edge as shown.

Foundation Piecing. Paper or fabric foundation pieces are used to make very accurate blocks, provide stability for weak fabrics, and add body and weight to the finished quilt. These are especially helpful when sewing the *Hexagonal Comfort* design (Page 29) or very small Log Cabin blocks like those used in *Log Cabin in the Woods* on Page 137.

Temporary foundation materials include paper, tracing paper, freezer paper and removable interfacing. Permanent foundations include utility fabrics, non-woven interfacing, flannel, fleece and batting.

Methods of marking foundations include basting lines, pencils or pens, needlepunching, tracing wheel, hot-iron transfers, copy machine, pre-marked, stamps or stencils.

There are two methods of foundation piecing—under piecing and top piecing. When underpiecing, the pattern is reversed when tracing. ***Note:*** *All patterns for which we recommend paper piecing are already reversed in full-size drawings given.*

Top piecing places the fabric pieces on top of the drawing which gives fabric placement lines instead of seam lines. For those who sew perfect 1/4" seams with no trouble, this method is easy. The *Log Cabin Twist* on Page 117 provides a pattern for top piecing. The lines on the drawing are not the seam lines, but are the placement lines for the edge of the fabric as shown in Figure 25.

To top-piece, align the edge of the fabric piece with the line on the foundation. Place presser foot at the end of the piece. Sew a perfect 1/4" seam along the piece. When stitching is complete, finger-press piece flat. It should line up with the next line. Continue adding pieces in numerical order until foundation or paper is covered.

To under-piece, place a scrap of fabric larger than the lined space on the unlined side of the paper in the No. 1 position. Place piece 2 right sides together with piece 1; pin on seam line, and fold back to check that the piece will cover space 2 before stitching.

Stitch along line on the lined side of the paper—fabric will not be visible. Sew several stitches beyond the beginning and ending of the line. Backstitching is not required as another fabric seam will cover this seam.

Remove pin; finger-press piece 2 flat. Continue adding all pieces in numerical order in the same manner until all pieces are stitched to paper. Trim excess to outside line (1/4" larger all around than finished size of the block).

Tracing paper can be used as a temporary foundation. It is removed when blocks are complete and stitched together. To paper-piece, copy patterns given here using a copy machine or trace each block individually. Measure the finished paper foundations to insure accuracy in copying.

Tips & Techniques

If you cannot see the lines on the backside of the paper when paper-piecing, draw over lines with a small felt-tip marker. The lines should now be visible on the backside to help with placement of fabric pieces.

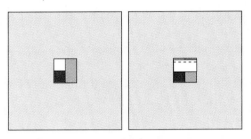

Figure 26
A fabric square was used as the foundation to which scrap patches were sewn.

Before machine-piecing fabric patches together, test your sewing machine for positioning an accurate 1/4" seam allowance. There are several tools to help guarantee this. Some machine needles may be moved to allow the presser-foot edge to be a 1/4" guide. A special foot may be purchased for your machine that will guarantee an accurate 1/4" seam. A piece of masking tape can be placed on the throat plate of your sewing machine to mark the 1/4" seam. A plastic stick-on ruler may be used instead of tape with the same results.

Putting It All Together

Many steps are required to prepare a quilt top for quilting, including setting the blocks together, adding borders, choosing and marking quilting designs, layering the top, batting and backing for quilting, the quilting or tying process and finishing the edges of the quilt.

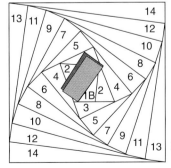

Figure 25
Lines on top-piecing pattern are lined up with edges of fabric piece.

As you begin the process of finishing your quilt top, strive for a neat, flat quilt with square sides and corners, not for perfection—that will come with time and practice.

Finishing the Top

Settings. Most Log Cabin quilts are made by sewing individual blocks together in rows which when joined create a design. There are several other methods used to join blocks, but most of these are not common to Log Cabin quilts.

Chimneys & Cornerstones on Page 47 uses sashing strips and squares to join the blocks. Sometimes the setting choice is determined by the block's design. For example, a house block should be placed upright on a quilt, not sideways or upside down (see *Miniature Log House* on Page 67).

Plain blocks can be alternated with pieced or appliquéd blocks in a straight set. Making a quilt using plain blocks saves time; half the number of pieced or appliquéd blocks are needed to make the same-size quilt.

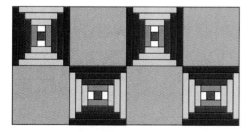

Figure 1
Alternate plain blocks with pieced blocks to save time making more pieced or appliquéd blocks.

Adding Borders. Borders are an integral part of the quilt and should complement the colors and designs used in the quilt center. Borders frame a quilt just like a mat and frame do a picture.

If fabric strips are added for borders, they may be mitered or butted at the corners as shown in Figures 2 and 3. To determine the size for butted border strips, measure across the center of the completed quilt top from one side raw edge to the other side raw edge. This measurement will include a 1/4" seam allowance.

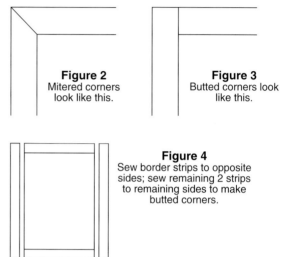

Figure 2
Mitered corners look like this.

Figure 3
Butted corners look like this.

Figure 4
Sew border strips to opposite sides; sew remaining 2 strips to remaining sides to make butted corners.

Cut two border strips that length by the chosen width of the border. Sew these strips to the top and bottom of the pieced center referring to Figure 4. Press the seam allowance toward border strips.

Measure across the completed quilt top at the center, from top raw edge to bottom raw edge, including the two border strips added. Cut two border strips that length by the chosen width of the border. Sew a strip to the two remaining sides as shown in Figure 4. Press the seams toward border strips.

Carefully press the entire piece, including the pieced center. Avoid pulling and stretching while pressing, which would distort shapes.

To make mitered corners, measure the quilt as before. Double the width of the border and add seam allowance to determine the length of the strips. Repeat for opposite sides. Sew on each strip, stopping stitching 1/4" from corner, leaving the remainder of the strip dangling.

Sew on all four strips. Press corners at a 45-degree angle to form a crease. Stitch from the inside quilt corner to the outside on the creased line. Trim excess away after stitching and press mitered seams open (Figures 5–7).

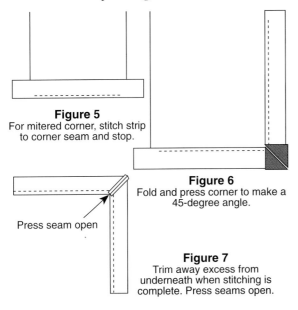

Figure 5
For mitered corner, stitch strip to corner seam and stop.

Figure 6
Fold and press corner to make a 45-degree angle.

Press seam open

Figure 7
Trim away excess from underneath when stitching is complete. Press seams open.

Getting Ready to Quilt
Choosing a Quilting Design. If you choose to hand- or machine-quilt your finished top, you will need to select a design for quilting. Manufactured quilt-design templates are available in many designs and sizes and are cut out of a durable plastic template material which is easy to use.

There are several types of quilting designs, some of which may not have to be marked. The easiest of the unmarked designs is in-the-ditch quilting. Many Log Cabin quilts are quilted in this method. Here the quilting stitches are placed in the valley created by the seams joining two pieces together or next to the edge of an appliqué design. There is no need to mark a top for in-the-ditch quilting. Machine quilters

choose this option because the stitches are not as obvious on the finished quilt. (Figure 8).

Outline-quilting 1/4" or more away from seams or appliqué shapes is another no-mark alternative (Figure 9) which helps one avoid having to sew through the layers made by seams, thus making stitching easier.

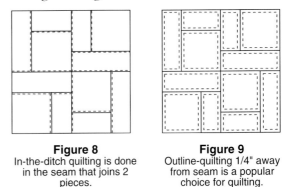

Figure 8
In-the-ditch quilting is done in the seam that joins 2 pieces.

Figure 9
Outline-quilting 1/4" away from seam is a popular choice for quilting.

If you are not comfortable eyeballing the 1/4" (or other distance), masking tape is available in different widths and is helpful to place on straight-edge designs to mark the quilting line. If using masking tape, place the tape right up against the seam and quilt close to the other edge.

Meander or free-motion quilting by machine fills in open spaces and doesn't require marking. It is fun and easy to stitch.

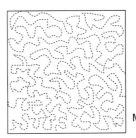

Figure 10
Machine meander quilting fills in large spaces.

Marking the Top for Quilting or Tying. If you choose a fancy or allover design for quilting, you will need to transfer the design to your quilt top before layering with the backing and batting. You may use a sharp medium-lead or silver pencil on light background fabrics. Test the pencil marks to guarantee that they will wash out of your quilt top when quilting is complete; or be sure your quilting stitches cover the pencil marks. Mechanical pencils with very fine points or special washable markers may be used successfully to mark quilts.

To make a permanent quilt-design template, choose a template material with which to transfer the design. See-through plastic is the best as it will let you place the design while allowing you to see where it is in relation to your quilt design without moving it. Place the design on the quilt top where you want it and trace around it with your marking tool. Pick up the quilting template and place again; repeat marking.

No matter what marking method you use, remember—the marked lines should *never show* on the finished quilt. When the top is marked, it is ready for layering.

Preparing the Quilt Backing. The quilt backing is a very important feature of your quilt. In most cases, the Materials list for each quilt in this book gives the size requirements for the backing, not the yardage needed. Exceptions to this are when the backing fabric is also used on the quilt top and yardage is given for that fabric.

A backing is generally cut at least 4" larger than the quilt top or 2" larger on all sides. For a 64" x 78" finished quilt, the backing would need to be at least 68" x 82".

To avoid having the seam across the center of the quilt backing, cut or tear one of the right-length pieces in half and sew half to each side of the second piece as shown in Figure 11.

Quilts that need a backing more than 88" wide may be pieced in horizontal pieces as shown in Figure 12.

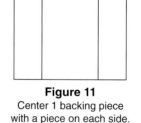

Figure 11
Center 1 backing piece
with a piece on each side.

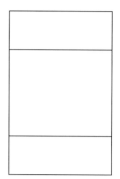

Figure 12
Horizontal seams may be
used on backing pieces.

Layering the Quilt Sandwich. Layering the quilt top with the batting and backing is time-consuming. Open the batting several days before you need it and place over a bed or flat on the floor to help flatten the creases caused from its being folded up in the bag for so long.

Iron the backing piece, folding in half both vertically and horizontally and pressing to mark centers.

If you will not be quilting on a frame, place the backing right side down on a clean floor or table. Start in the center and push any wrinkles or bunches flat. Use masking tape to tape the edges to the floor or large clips to hold the backing to the edge of the table. The backing should be taut.

Place the batting on top of the backing, matching centers using fold lines as guides; flatten out any wrinkles. Trim the batting to the same size as the backing.

Fold the quilt top in half lengthwise and place on top of the batting, wrong side against the batting, matching centers. Unfold quilt and, working from the center to the outside edges, smooth out any wrinkles or lumps.

To hold the quilt layers together for quilting, baste by hand or use safety pins. If basting by hand, thread a long thin needle with a long piece of unknotted white or off-white thread. Starting in the center and leaving a long tail, make 4"–6" stitches toward the outside edge of the quilt top, smoothing as you baste. Start at the center again and work toward the outside as shown in Figure 13.

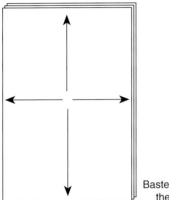

Figure 13
Baste from the center to the outside edges.

If quilting by machine, you may prefer to use safety pins for holding your fabric sandwich together. Start in the center of the quilt and pin to the outside, leaving pins open until all are placed. When you are satisfied that all layers are smooth, close the pins.

Quilting

Hand Quilting. Hand quilting is the process of placing stitches through the quilt top, batting and backing to hold them together. While it is a functional process, it also adds beauty and loft to the finished quilt.

To begin, thread a sharp between needle with an 18" piece of quilting thread. Tie a small knot in the end of the thread. Position the needle about 1/2" to 1" away from the starting point on quilt top. Sink the needle through the top into the batting layer but not through the backing. Pull the needle up at the starting point of the quilting design. Pull the needle and thread until the knot sinks through the top into the batting (Figure 14).

Some stitchers like to take a backstitch here at the beginning while others prefer to begin the first stitch here. Take small, even running stitches along the marked quilting line (Figure 15). Keep one hand positioned underneath to feel the needle go all the way through to the backing.

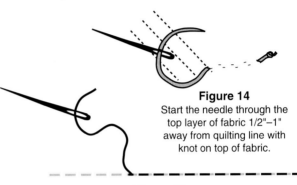

Figure 14
Start the needle through the top layer of fabric 1/2"–1" away from quilting line with knot on top of fabric.

Figure 15
Make small, even running stitches on marked quilting line.

Tips & Techniques

Knots should not show on the quilt top or back. Learn to sink the knot into the batting at the beginning and ending of the quilting thread for successful stitches. Making 12–18 stitches per inch is a wonderful goal, but a more realistic goal is seven to nine stitches per inch. If you cannot accomplish this right away, strive for even stitches—all the same size—that look as good on the back as on the front.

When you have nearly run out of thread, wind the thread around the needle several times to make a small knot and pull it close to the fabric. Insert the needle into the fabric on the quilting line and come out with the needle 1/2" to 1" away, pulling the knot into the fabric layers the same as when you started. Pull and cut thread close to fabric. The end should disappear inside after cutting. Some quilters prefer to take a backstitch with a loop through it for a knot to end.

You will perfect your quilting stitches as you gain experience and your stitches will get better with each project and your style will be uniquely your own.

Tips & Techniques

Hand quilting can produce very sore fingers and strain to muscles in the hand, arm and shoulder. To prevent sore fingers, use a thimble. The finger that is under the quilt to feel the needle as it passes through the backing is the one that is most apt to get sore from the pin pricks. Some quilters purchase leather thimbles for this finger while others try home remedies. One simple aid is masking tape wrapped around the finger. With the tape you will still be able to feel the needle, but it will not prick your skin. Over time calluses build up and these fingers get toughened up, but with every vacation from quilting, they will become soft and the process begins again.

If you feel your muscles tensing up, take a rest. It is possible to develop serious problems such as carpel tunnel syndrome in the hands or wrists and muscle spasms in the shoulders. These conditions can be permanent and require medical attention.

Machine Quilting. Successful machine quilting requires practice and a good relationship with your sewing machine to find success.

Prepare the quilt for machine quilting in the same way as for hand-quilting. Use safety pins to hold the layers together instead of basting with thread.

Presser-foot quilting is best used for straight-line quilting because the presser bar lever does not need to be continually lifted.

Set the machine on a longer stitch length (three or eight to 10 stitches to the inch). Too tight a stitch causes puckering and fabric tucks, either on the quilt top or backing. An even-feed or walking foot helps to eliminate the tucks and puckering by feeding the upper and lower lay-

ers through the machine evenly. Before you begin, loosen the amount of pressure on the presser foot.

Special machine-quilting needles work best to penetrate the three layers in your quilt.

Decide on a design. Quilting in the ditch is not quite as visible, but if you quilt with the feed dogs engaged, it means turning the quilt frequently. It is not easy to fit a rolled-up quilt through the small opening on the sewing machine head.

Meander quilting is the easiest way to machine-quilt—and it is fun. Meander quilting is done using an appliqué or darning foot with the feed dogs dropped. It is sort of like scribbling. Simply move the quilt top around under the foot and make stitches in a random pattern to fill the space. The same method may be used to outline a quilt design. The trick is the same as in hand-quilting; you are striving for stitches of uniform size. Your hands are in complete control of the design.

If machine-quilting is of interest to you, there are several very good books available at quilt shops that will help you become a successful machine quilter.

Tied Quilts, or Comforters. Would you rather tie your quilt layers together than quilt them? Tied quilts are often referred to as comforters. The advantage of tying is that it takes so much less time and the required skills can be learned quickly.

If a top will be tied, choose a thick, bonded batting—one that will not separate during washing. For tying, use pearl cotton, embroidery floss, or strong yarn in colors that match or coordinate with the fabrics in your quilt top.

Decide on a pattern for tying. Many quilts are tied at the corners and centers of the blocks and at sashing joints. Try to tie every 4"–6". Special designs can be used for tying, but most quilts are tied in conventional ways. Begin tying in the center and work to the outside edges.

To make the tie, thread a large needle with a long thread (yarn, floss or crochet cotton); do not knot. Push the needle through the quilt top to the back, leaving a 3"–4" length on top. Move the needle to the next position without cutting thread. Take another stitch through the layers; repeat until thread is almost used up.

Cut thread between stitches, leaving an equal amount of thread on each stitch. Tie a knot with the two thread ends. Tie again to make a square knot referring to Figure 16. Trim thread ends to desired length.

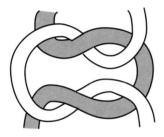

Figure 16
Make a square knot as shown.

Finishing the Edges

When your quilt is tied or quilted, the edges need to be finished. Decide how you want the edges of your quilt finished before layering the backing and batting with the quilt top.

Without Binding—Self-Finish. There is one way to eliminate adding an edge finish. This is done before quilting. Place the batting on a flat surface. Place the pieced top right side up on the batting. Place the backing right sides together with the pieced top. Pin and/or baste layers together to hold flat referring to Page 154.

Begin stitching in the center of one side using a 1/4" seam allowance, reversing at the beginning and end of the seam. Continue stitching all around and back to the beginning side. Leave a 12" or larger opening. Clip corners to reduce

excess. Turn right side out through the opening. Slipstitch the opening closed by hand. The quilt may now be quilted by hand or machine.

The disadvantage to this method is that once the edges are sewn in, any creases or wrinkles that might form during the quilting process cannot be flattened out. Tying is the preferred method of finishing a quilt constructed using this method.

Bringing the backing fabric to the front is another way to finish the quilt's edge without binding. To accomplish this, complete the quilt as for hand or machine quilting. Trim the batting *only* even with the front. Trim the backing 1" larger than the completed top all around.

Turn the backing edge in 1/2" and then turn over to the front along edge of batting. The folded edge may be machine-stitched close to the edge through all layers, or blind-stitched in place to finish.

The front may be turned to the back. If using this method, a wider front border is needed. The backing and batting are trimmed 1" *smaller* than the top and the top edge is turned under 1/2" and then turned to the back and stitched in place.

One more method of self-finish may be used. The top and backing may be stitched together by hand at the edge. To accomplish this, all quilting must be stopped 1/2" from the quilt-top edge. The top and backing of the quilt are trimmed even and the batting is trimmed to 1/4"–1/2" smaller. The edges of the top and backing are turned in 1/4"–1/2" and blind-stitched together at the very edge.

These methods do not require the use of extra fabric and save time in preparation of binding strips; they are not as durable as an added binding.

Binding. The technique of adding extra fabric at the edges of the quilt is called binding. The binding encloses the edges and adds an extra layer of fabric for durability.

To prepare the quilt for the addition of the binding, trim the batting and backing layers flush with the top of the quilt using a rotary cutter and ruler or shears. Using a walking-foot attachment (sometimes called an even-feed foot attachment), machine-baste the three layers together all around approximately 1/8" from the cut edge.

The list of materials given with each quilt in this book often includes a number of yards of self-made or purchased binding. Bias binding may be purchased in packages and in many colors. The advantage to self-made binding is that you can use fabrics from your quilt to coordinate colors.

Double-fold, straight-grain binding and double-fold, bias-grain binding are two of the most commonly used types of binding.

Double-fold, straight-grain binding is used on smaller projects with right-angle corners. Double-fold, bias-grain binding is best suited for bed-size quilts or quilts with rounded corners.

To make double-fold, straight-grain binding, cut 2"-wide strips of fabric across the width or down the length of the fabric totaling the perimeter of the quilt plus 10". The strips are joined as shown in Figure 17 and pressed in half wrong sides together along the length using an iron on a cotton setting with *no* steam.

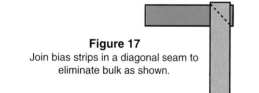

Figure 17
Join bias strips in a diagonal seam to eliminate bulk as shown.

Lining up the raw edges, place the binding on the top of the quilt and begin sewing (again

using the walking foot) approximately 6" from the beginning of the binding strip. Stop sewing 1/4" from the first corner, leave the needle in the quilt, turn and sew diagonally to the corner as shown in Figure 18.

Fold the binding at a 45-degree angle up and away from the quilt as shown in Figure 19 and back down flush with the raw edges. Starting at the top raw edge of the quilt, begin sewing the next side as shown in Figure 20. Repeat at the next three corners.

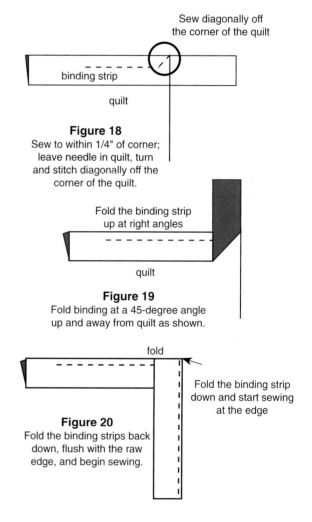

Figure 18
Sew to within 1/4" of corner; leave needle in quilt, turn and stitch diagonally off the corner of the quilt.

Figure 19
Fold binding at a 45-degree angle up and away from quilt as shown.

Figure 20
Fold the binding strips back down, flush with the raw edge, and begin sewing.

As you approach the beginning of the binding strip, stop stitching and overlap the binding

1/2" from the edge; trim. Join the two ends with a 1/4" seam allowance and press the seam open. Reposition the joined binding along the edge of the quilt and resume stitching to the beginning.

To finish, bring the folded edge of the binding over the raw edges and blind-stitch the binding in place over the machine-stitching line on the backside. Hand-miter the corners on the back as shown in Figure 21.

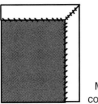

Figure 21
Miter and stitch
corners as shown.

If you are making a quilt to be used on a bed, you will want to use double-fold, bias-grain bindings because the many threads that cross each other along the fold at the edge of the quilt make it a more durable binding.

Cut 2"-wide bias strips from a large square of fabric. Join the strips as illustrated in Figure 17 and press the seams open. Fold the beginning end of the bias strip 1/4" from the raw edge and press. Fold the joined strips in half along the long side, wrong sides together, and press with *no* steam (Figure 22).

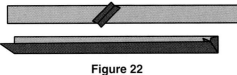

Figure 22
Fold end in and press strip in half.

Follow the same procedures as previously described for preparing the quilt top and sewing the binding to the quilt top. Treat the corners just as you treated them with straight-grain binding.

Since you are using bias-grain binding, you do

have the option to just eliminate the corners if this option doesn't interfere with the patchwork in the quilt. Round the corners off by placing one of your dinner plates at the corner and rotary-cutting the gentle curve (Figure 23).

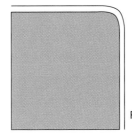

Figure 23
Round corners to eliminate
square-corner finishes.

As you approach the beginning of the bias strip, stop stitching and lay the end across the beginning so it will slip inside the fold. Cut the end at a 45-degree angle so the raw edges are contained inside the beginning of the strip (Figure 24). Resume stitching to the beginning. Bring the fold to the back of the quilt and hand-stitch as previously described.

Figure 24
End the binding strips as shown.

Overlapped corners are not quite as easy as rounded ones, but a bit easier than mitering. To make overlapped corners, sew binding strips to opposite sides of the quilt top. Stitch edges down to finish. Trim ends even.

Sew a strip to each remaining side, leaving 1 1/2"–2" excess at each end. Turn quilt over and fold binding down even with previous finished edge as shown in Figure 25.

Fold binding in toward quilt and stitch down as before, enclosing the previous bound edge in the seam. It may be necessary to trim the folded-down section to reduce bulk.

Figure 25
Fold end of binding even
with previous edge.

Figure 26
An overlapped corner
is not quite as neat as
a mitered corner.

Final Touches

If your quilt will be hung on the wall, a hanging sleeve is required. Other options include purchased plastic rings or fabric tabs. The best choice is a fabric sleeve which will evenly distribute the weight of the quilt across the top edge rather than at selected spots where tabs or rings are stitched and keep the quilt hanging straight and not damage the batting.

To make a sleeve, measure across the top of the finished quilt. Cut an 8" piece of muslin equal to that length—you may need to seam several muslin strips together to make the required length.

Fold in 1/4" on each end of the muslin strip and press. Fold again and stitch to hold. Fold the muslin strip lengthwise with right sides together. Sew along the long side to make a

tube. Turn the tube right side out; press with seam at bottom or centered on the back.

Hand-stitch the tube along the top of the quilt and the bottom of the tube to the quilt back making sure the quilt lies flat. Stitches should not go through to the front of the quilt and don't need to be too close together.

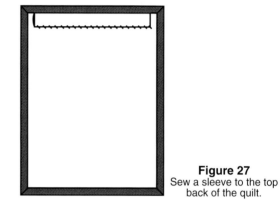

Figure 27
Sew a sleeve to the top
back of the quilt.

Slip a wooden dowel or long curtain rod through the sleeve to hang.

When the quilt is finally complete, it should be signed and dated. Use a permanent pen on the back of the quilt. Other methods include cross-stitching your name and date on the front or back or making a permanent label which may be stitched to the back.

Acknowledgments

Special thanks to the following for photography on location: Adams County Courthouse, Decatur, Ind., Page 9; Habegger Furniture, Inc., Berne, Ind., Page 98; Hans Bed & Breakfast, Berne, Ind., Pages 110, 122, 126; Limberlost State Historical Site, Geneva, Ind., Pages 7, 78–79, 88, 94; Schug House Inn, Berne, Ind., Pages 6, 16, 24; Swiss Heritage Village, Berne, Ind., Page 28; and Swiss Village Retirement Community, Berne, Ind., Page 54.

The antique quilts on Pages 6–9, "An American Tradition," are shown courtesy of Xenia Cord, Legacy Quilts, Kokomo, Ind.